Landmark Visitors Guide

Arran,
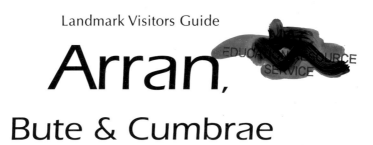

Bute & Cumbrae

Ro

D1188070

Ron Scholes is an author, landscape photographer and travel
lecturer. He has been a regular contributor to countryside
programmes for BBC local radio, and to the *Yorkshire Journal* and
Outdoor Pursuits magazines. His latest books have included, *The
Ravenber, a Coast to Coast Walk*, and *Towns and Villages of
Britain – Cheshire*.

Ron is a retired Headteacher, and a former long-serving leader for
Youth Hostels Association Walking Tours at home and abroad. He
has completed many of the long distance walks in the UK,
including routes from Cape Wrath to Lands End.

Ron Scholes
Master of Education: Diploma of Advanced Study in Education:
Fellow of the Royal Geographical Society (FRGS):
Chartered Geographer (C. Geog): Member. Outdoor Writers' Guild.
Ron Scholes email: ron.scholes@btinternet.com

Published by
Landmark Publishing
Ashbourne Hall, Cokayne Ave, Ashbourne,
Derbyshire DE6 1EJ England

Acknowledgements

Re. Page 4: The Puffers quotations from Para Handy by Neil Munro.
Birlinn Limited, West Newington House, 10 Newington Road,
Edinburgh EH9 1QS www.birlinn.co.uk

Right: Glen Rosa, Arran.

Landmark Visitors Guide

Arran,
Bute & Cumbrae

Ron Scholes

Published in the UK by
Landmark Publishing Ltd,
Ashbourne Hall, Cokayne Avenue, Ashbourne, Derbyshire DE6 1EJ England
Tel: (01335) 347349 Fax: (01335) 347303
e-mail: sales@landmarkpublishing.co.uk
website: landmarkpublishing.co.uk

Published in the USA by
Hunter Publishing Inc,
130 Campus Drive, Edison NJ 08818
Tel: (732) 225 1900, (800) 255 0343 Fax: (732) 417 0482
website: www.hunterpublishing.com

ISBN 13: 978-1-84306-213-4

ISBN 10: 1-84306-213-5

Print: Biddles Ltd, King's Lynn Norfolk
Design & Cartography: Mark Titterton

Front cover: Glen Rosa, Arran.
Back cover, top: Rothesay Castle, Bute.

photographs: Ron Scholes and C.L.M. Porter.

Contents

THE WALKING ROUTES

The routes described present no technical difficulties in good summer weather. However for experienced walkers, routes in the higher mountains and hills sometimes involve hands-on scrambling. Care should be taken on the granite ridges where there is path erosion; and on bouldery slopes or on tussocky moorlands.

Wear boots and carry a map and compass at all times. Motto – 'watch where you are putting your feet!'

The combined contribution of the islands in the Firth of Clyde to the glory of this lovely stretch of water is undeniable. Lying close to Scotland's central heartland, Arran, Great Cumbrae and Bute are all very accessible from the mainland. The common routes by rail are from Glasgow to Ardrossan for the Isle of Arran; to Largs for Great Cumbrae, and to Wemyss Bay for the Isle of Bute. The island of Little Cumbrae is privately owned, but with a recent new owner, it is hoped that the island will become more accessible. For access to Ailsa Craig, there are boat trips, by arrangement, from Girvan.

APPROACH TO THE ISLANDS

However, a visitor intent on exploring these islands in the Firth of Clyde, has a splendid opportunity of gaining a landscape bonus, long before Ailsa Craig or Arran come into view. This is the approach by road, particularly the routes taken by motorists from the direction of northern England. There is no finer journey than by following the beautiful coastline of Dumfries and Galloway, and through the glens and rugged hills of south-west Scotland.

OVERVIEW OF THE ISLANDS

Further up on the coast, and lying 15 miles (24 km) across the water, is the exciting outline of the Isle of Arran. There are lofty and jagged mountains in the north gashed by narrow glens, with Goatfell, 2,866 ft (874m) the highest point.

The northern granite peaks were formed by volcanic intrusions, when great masses of magma pushed through the surrounding sedimentary rocks. In central Arran, the rounded hills are less dramatic than the north, the volcano here being smaller and eroded down to its lower part. Here, the igneous rocks contain masses of fragments of various kinds of rock.

To the south, the underlying New Red Sandstones, and areas of volcanic intrusions containing quartz and quartz-free rocks, form an undulating landscape of moorland patched by afforestation, and cut by many watercourses. The land slopes down to a coastline of caves and raised beaches. Here, rocky dykes run out to sea, with sandy areas in between, facing the low-lying islet of Pladda. The south-eastern coastline is broken by the steep bulk of Holy Island.

For the walker, there is fine hill and ridge, coastal, and glen scenery; for cyclists and motorists, pleasant roads run around and across the island. The Arran circular road, which is 56 miles (89.6km) long, mostly hugs the coastline except in the north and south, and for two short lengths in the east and west. Two minor roads, The String and The Ross, cross the island from east to west; 10 miles (16km) and 8 miles (12.8m) long respectively.

There are numerous Neolithic and Bronze Age monuments to seek out and explore; such as standing stones, hut circles, burial chambers and stone circles, as well as Iron Age forts. The Clearances at the beginning of the nineteenth century left their mark in the Arran Glens: for example, Sannox, Catacol and Sliddery to name but a few.

Closer to the mainland, and set out like stepping stones to the Island of Bute in the Firth of Clyde, lie the small islands of Little Cumbrae, "Wee" Cumbrae as it is sometimes called, and Great Cumbrae. The former, infrequently visited, is rugged with rock outcrops and raised beaches. The island is worth a geological study; it is mainly formed of Carboniferous volcanic rocks, after large fissure volcanoes covered the area in a sequence of basalt lava flows. The highest point is The Cairn on Lighthouse Hill, 403ft (123m), and close by the ancient lighthouse tower built in 1757.

The island of Great Cumbrae is basically a green ridge underlain by Old Red Sandstone rocks, with a band of limestone around Millport. However, there are many igneous dykes with wall-like features, such as "The Lion" near the south-east corner opposite Largs, and the Deil's Dyke near Keppel Pier, also on the east. The highest point on the island is the Glaid Stone on Barbay Hill, 416ft (127m). The B896 road that runs round the shoreline is 10.5 miles (16.8km) long.

In the south, the attractive resort of Millport has a surprise in store – a Cathedral of the Isles. Many visitors seem unaware of the existence of the little Cathedral, because it is situated among trees behind the town.

The Isle of Bute lies to the west and to the north-west of the Cumbraes. The larger part of the northern area is made up of Highland quartzites and schists, and in the southern part below the Highland Boundary Fault, there are Old Red Sandstone and Carboniferous volcanic rocks. The underlying geology dictates the nature of the landscape. To the north are craggy hills and heather-covered moorland, divided from a similar type of countryside by a low-lying farming belt. The fault line is occupied by a number of freshwater lochs, and south of the Boundary Fault, it is the more gentle fertile scenery of softer sedimentary and volcanic rocks. The island is also fortunate in having a number of quiet sandy bays like Ettrick Bay.

Rothesay with its castle is the main town; its Esplanade Gardens house the Discovery Centre. To the south of the Royal Burgh, stands Mount Stuart House featuring magnificent Victorian Gothic architecture and design. This award-winning attraction is set in 300-acre (120ha) grounds, with various gardens, and splendid vistas of the Firth of Clyde.

There is an excellent walking route around the island, cleverly described as the West Island Way – Scotland's first long distance island footpath – distance, a modest 30 miles (48km).

The visitor approaching the islands in the Firth of Clyde for the first time may catch a glimpse of the striking outline of the Arran hills, or the gentler profiles of Bute and the Cumbraes. Then their visual impact is astounding. However, too often, the islands become black smudges beneath a curtain of rain and cloud. Nevertheless, let there be a north-west wind, and their contribution to the glory of the Firth of Clyde cannot be denied. Other viewpoints can be just as breathtaking: on a summer morning looking towards Loch Striven and the hills of Cowal on the ferry crossing to Rothesay; or from Dunagoil in southern Bute across to the sunlit peaks and corries of northern Arran; or on an autumn afternoon from the ridge of Torr Mór, also in southern Bute, as the golden light bathes the rugged west coast of Little Cumbrae. At sunset, on a winter evening, the view across Millport Bay on Great Cumbrae to the silhouetted outline of the Arran peaks is unforgettable.

Ailsa Craig

As a taster for the lovely islands to come, this impressive rock rearing out of the sea is the core of an ancient volcano. It is known locally as Paddy's Milestone, because of its position midway between Glasgow and Ireland. Its dome-like shape attains a height of 1,109 ft (338m), and is thought to be the basal remains of a volcanic vent. This created towering cliffs with some columnar pillars 400ft (122m) in height. The acid igneous rock has been cut through by dolerite dykes, and it is alongside these that the majority of caves are to be found. There is a distinctive seam of a fine-grained micro-granite in the north-west and in the south of the island. This mineral, riebeckite, became famous for making quality curling stones that were cut on the island.

Ailsa Craig is also well known for its varied bird population, particularly recognised for its immense gannet colony. At one time there was also a large puffin colony, but the presence of a large number of brown rats devouring their eggs forced the puffins to leave. However, a programme of rat eradication took place in 1991 when tons of poison was laid down. Happily, since 2002, puffins have started to re-establish their nest-burrows. Other species nesting on this remote rocky dome are guillemots, shelduck, gulls and kittiwakes.

Although barren in appearance, the island is well covered with flowers, noticeably on the upper slopes. There are the white flowers of scurvy grass, red lychnis and the tree mallow, *lavatera arborea*.

The lighthouse, which has functioned since 1886, is now automatically operated. There is a huddle of buildings round the lighthouse, and the remains of a narrow-gauge railway track runs to the abandoned quarry on the southern side of the island.

It is worth attempting the clear path that zig-zags up to the ruins of the old square peel tower, which had three storeys, and displays the coat of arms of three stars of the Hamilton family. The path proceeds below crags to tiny Garra Loch, and continues its airy way across great rock slabs, to swing round and up to the OS column at the summit. Given good conditions, there are superb all round views. The island can easily be explored in a day. Camping is possible by the lighthouse, but ensure that spare food is taken as bad weather could cause an extended stay. Enquire for permission to camp from the Cassillis Estates.

Access to the island is by boat trip (contact ☎01465 713219 or mccrindlem@aol.com). It is 10 miles (16km) from Girvan, and the crossing time is approximately one hour.

2. Isle of Arran

Arran, scarcely two hours' journey from Scotland's populated heartland, is an island of many attractions and great scenic contrasts. It lies some 15 miles (24km) west of the Ayrshire coastline, and dominates the approaches to the Firth of Clyde and the entrance to Loch Fyne. It is sheltered to the west by Kintyre, from which it is separated by the Kilbrannan Sound.

The landscape of the northern part of the island is in marked contrast to the southern part, principally due to the underlying geological structures which give Arran a character of its own. The island is 19 miles (30.4km) long from the Cock of Arran in the north to Bennan Head in the south, and 10 miles (16km) wide from Machrie Bay in the west to Corrygills Point in the east. Its 165 sq.miles (427 sq.km), is split almost equally by the Highland Boundary Fault, giving rise to geology and scenery akin to the Highlands in the north, and to the Scottish Lowlands in the south.

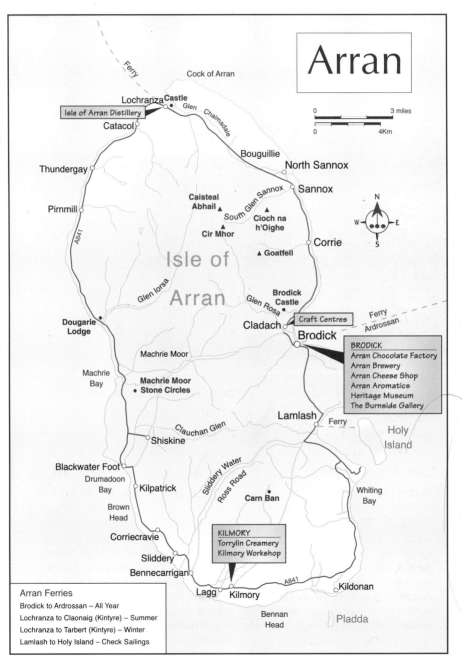

Arran

0 _____ 3 miles
0 _____ 4Km

- Cock of Arran
- Lochranza Castle
- **Isle of Arran Distillery**
- Catacol
- Glen Chalmadale
- Bouguillie
- North Sannox
- Thundergay
- South Glen Sannox
- Sannox
- **Caisteal Abhail** ▲
- Pirnmill
- A841
- Cioch na h'Oighe ▲
- **Cir Mhor** ▲
- Corrie
- ▲ Goatfell
- Isle of Arran
- Glen Iorsa
- **Brodick Castle**
- Glen Rosa
- Ferry Ardrossan
- **Dougarie Lodge**
- Craft Centres
- Cladach
- **Brodick**
- Machrie Moor
- **BRODICK**
  Arran Chocolate Factory
  Arran Brewery
  Arran Cheese Shop
  Arran Aromatics
  Heritage Museum
  The Burnside Gallery
- Machrie Bay
- **Machrie Moor**
  • Stone Circles
- Lamlash
- Ferry
- Holy Island
- Clauchan Glen
- Shiskine
- Sliddery Water
- Ross Road
- Blackwater Foot
- Drumadoon Bay
- **Kilpatrick**
- **Carn Ban** •
- Whiting Bay
- Brown Head
- Corriecravie
- **KILMORY**
  Torrylin Creamery
  Kilmory Workshop
- Sliddery
- Bennecarrigan
- A841
- Kildonan
- Lagg
- Kilmory
- Bennan Head
- Pladda

Arran Ferries

Brodick to Ardrossan – All Year
Lochranza to Claonaig (Kintyre) – Summer
Lochranza to Tarbert (Kintyre) – Winter
Lamlash to Holy Island – Check Sailings

From records, it appears that the first holidaymakers came to Arran in the first part of the eighteenth century in order to drink goat's milk and to ramble in the glens near to Brodick. At the beginning of the nineteenth century, the scenery was described in verse and prose, and no doubt stimulated interest in the island. This new awareness developed into a fashion for open-air holidays; such as scrambles on the peaks, walks to remote spots, picnics in the glens and inshore fishing.

Early steam paddle boat services started in the first part of the nineteenth century from Greenock and Glasgow, and from Adrossan a little later. There was a great deal of competition between the boat companies and much amalgamation of railways. Turbine-powered boats appeared in 1901, until the introduction in 1957 of a motor vessel, the *Glen Sannox*, with a car deck and lift. Brodick pier was the first to be built on the island, followed by piers at Lamlash, Lochranza and Whiting Bay. It is interesting to note, that in the progress from sail to steam, the first Arran puffer, *Glencloy*, was built on the island and launched in 1895.

As the means of transport to the island improved, so did accommodation. In the mid-nineteenth century, some villas and terraces of houses were built. In the days of the 12th Duke, the tenants were allowed to take in visitors, provided they paid an increase in the rent. The same Duke had restricted building on the island, but after his death in 1895, many of the red sandstone villas, shops, and boarding houses were constructed around the island.

BRODICK AND NORTH-EAST ARRAN

The large village of **Brodick** lies on the south edge of the bay, but the original settlement was on the north side. Today, its main features and facilities lie along the road on the way to the ferry terminal. Approaching from the north end there is the Church of Scotland on a side road, and Brodick Golf Club facing Ormidale Park. Other facilities include: the library, post office, fire station, supermarket, bowling green, Bank of Scotland, mountain bike hire, craft shop and bakery. There are ample parking spaces along the road, together with hotels and guest houses looking out to Brodick Bay. In the grounds of the Douglas Hotel is the *Arran Banner* newspaper office. There is a Roman Catholic church, a mountain rescue post and the Brodick Pharmacy with a digital photo lab. At the Caledonian MacBrayne ferry terminal, there is the Tourist Information Centre, bus station and office and filling station.

AROUND BRODICK

The Isle of Arran Brewery with shop and Visitor Centre is located at **Cladach**, 2 miles (3.2km) north of Brodick and close to Brodick Castle. There is a convenient footpath to the brewery alongside Brodick Beach. The centre has a range of ales, gift packs and souvenirs. There are tours and tasters at any time, with easy access for people with disabilities. Cladach has been developed as the Arran Craft Centre featuring a range of arts and crafts. Also, on the craft trail is the **Burnside Gallery** in Auchrannie Road, Brodick. The gallery exhibits work by artists and craftsmen on the island. There is a frequently-changing, exhibition programme of mixed media work.

At Rosaburn, on the main road, just north of Brodick, is the Arran Heritage Museum. Its extensive presentations are very informative including, genealogy, archaeology, archival material, the Vikings, geology and a nineteenth-century cottage. School parties are welcome, and children can enjoy the many "hands on" exhibits. After viewing, there is the café or picnic area by the riverside.

Also easily approachable on the coast and north of Brodick, or by footpath alongside Brodick beach, is the **Island Cheese Company**. There is a viewing area, and the factory shop offers tasting of samples – try the Goat Fell crotins, or some Arran Blue. After visiting the cheese shop, pop into the wonderfully scented Arran Aromatics, where there are unique and beautifully packaged handmade soaps and beauty products.

Situated in the heart of Brodick is the **Arran Chocolate factory**, with a mouthwatering range of luxury chocolates and fresh cream truffles.

BRODICK CASTLE, GARDENS AND COUNTRY PARK

The entrance to Brodick Castle and Gardens (National Trust for Scotland) lies just 1½ miles (2.4km) north of the Arran Heritage Centre, off the coastal road A841. The castle, which overlooks Brodick Bay, is backed by Goatfell, and is surrounded by woodlands and fine gardens. The building is reputed to be the oldest habitable property belonging to the National Trust for Scotland, and the earliest parts date back to the fourteenth century. For the greater part of its history, it was owned by the Hamilton family, who acquired the estate and title of the Earls of Arran in 1503.

Little of the castle's medieval work can now be identified, but most likely, the building belongs to three main periods. A sixteenth-century tower house forms the central part, on to which Cromwell's garrison added an extra wing and an artillery battery. The largest section was built in 1844, in what can be termed the Scottish Baronial style, which blends in well with the older parts of the building.

The interior of the house contains rich decorations and furnishings, and a large collection of Beckford's treasures. There is the long red gallery, with a row of austere straight-backed chairs, the gracious drawing room with a fine plasterwork ceiling and elegant furniture. Look for the striking porcelain goose tureens, one of which carries an eel in its mouth, while the other holds a fish; and the part-panelled dining room situated in the sixteenth-century part of the castle, with its beautiful display of porcelain and silver.

The gardens at Brodick are outstanding and they account for much of the estate's attraction. The pond and woodland areas contain a comprehensive collection of rhododendron species, a sheltered walled garden is vibrant with colourful borders of herbaceous

Brodick Castle.

plants, and extensive well-manicured lawns are protected by trees and shrubs. Close by the pond garden is the Bavarian summer house, built about 1860; its ceiling and upper walls artistically decorated with pine cones.

A **Country Park** was established in 1980 and the Countryside Centre is part of a complex of buildings just above the castle. Here, noticeboards describe a number of nature trails that can be followed. The walks are colour-coded: Merkland Gorge – red; Castle Parks – blue; Cnocan – green and Lower Cnocan – yellow; another short stroll is Wilma's walk. Altogether there is a rich variety of landscape – woodland, forest clearings, waterfalls and bouldery burns. In the mixed woodland area there are many fine trees, including the rare Arran whitebeam, accompanied by a ground covering of wild garlic,

dog's mercury, ferns and bluebells. It is a special thrill to spot the red squirrels, which are numerous here, and an opportunity to study the varied bird life, which includes the peregrine falcon and the buzzard.

Near to the start of the walks is the walled Hamilton Cemetery. Here, slabs mark the graves of the 11th Duke and the 12th Duke and his wife.

ARRAN'S GRANITE PEAKS

The fine array of granite peaks in north-east Arran form the magnificent skyline that travellers see from across the Firth of Clyde, and in greater detail when approaching the island. The grey mountains are clustered around the highest point. **Goatfell**, 2,866ft (874m), and the serrated intervening ridges run out in all directions forming a splendid group of rugged summits. An evening sunset creates a wonderful silhouette of exciting dark outlines.

14

The convenient composition of these mountains allows walkers to complete circuits of varying lengths, and the great glens of Rosa and Sannox effectively split them into two halves, which allows easy access to the heart of the group.

The popularity of these mountains has created problems with erosion. This is particularly noticeable on the path up Goatfell, and down the steep north-west ridge of North Goatfell down to The Saddle. There is a section where the hard granite has been reduced to gritty, crumbling granite. With the exception of A'Chir and the Witch's Step, the ridges should not present any difficulty during the summer months, and will provide some very fine high-level walking. Where pinnacles and castellated tors exist, these can often be outflanked. However, during the winter months, these Arran mountains should not be underestimated. Mountain lovers will be impressed by the great rock faces, towering buttresses, and long extended slabs, or boiler plates of granite dropping slowly into the glens.

The distances given for walks, particularly in the hills, can only be calculated approximately from the maps. Due to the nature of the terrain, a map mile may in fact be considerably more. Naismith's formula used for hill walking in favourable conditions, allows one hour for each 3 map miles, plus half an hour for every 1,000 ft (305m) of ascent. Delays incurred because of bad weather are not included in the time allowed for reasonable stops.

WALKS IN NORTH-EAST ARRAN

WALK 1: Goatfell 2,866 ft (874m)
MAP: OS Explorer Sheet No: 361
DISTANCE: 6½ miles (10.4km)

Just south of the entrance to Brodick Castle, at Cladach, is the start of the walk up Goatfell, NS 012376; where there is a convenient car park. This is a straightforward route, crossing the exit driveway from Brodick Castle. Climb gradually through the rhododendrons on the red trail which branches off to the right into a plantation. Continue to ascend and follow the track that rises through bracken and heather to reach a small stream bridged by planks. Looking back, there is a fine view of Brodick Bay. Just ahead, pass through a gate in the deer fence, and walk up the steep path. Goatfell is clearly visible with the line of the pathway to the summit. Pass a series of cairns to reach the east ridge ahead. Finally, there is a steep ascent where the route winds round some large boulders. From the summit's survey pillar and direction indicator, there are excellent views of Cir Mhor and the neighbouring peaks; also of Glen Sannox to the north. One can return direct to the starting point by the same route.

WALK 2 Goatfell and Merkland Burn
MAP OS Explorer Sheet No: 361
DISTANCE: 8¹/₂ miles (13.6km)

On the return journey for WALK 1, the distance can be extended by descending by the same route until one reaches the marker for the red trail. Turn left and follow the Merkland Gorge Trail through Cnocan Wood to reach the Merkland Burn. Cross over the bridge and follow the burn downhill – note the small waterfalls. Turn right on to the forestry road, and cross over the burn on another bridge. Continue almost to the coast road, then bear right on to a path alongside parkland to reach Brodick Castle. Follow the driveway back to the Cladach car park.

WALK 3: Goatfell, The Saddle and Glen Rosa
MAP: OS Explorer Sheet No: 361
DISTANCE: 11 miles (17.6km)

This is a hard day's walk for experienced hill walkers. **Compass and map-reading skills essential**. It involves some steep and exposed rocky slopes, with some basic scrambling. The walk includes the summit of Goatfell, North Goatfell, The Saddle and the long tramp down Glen Rosa.

From the Cladach car park proceed as for WALK 1 to the summit of Goatfell. Follow the jumbled bouldery Stacach ridge, where the rocky tors can be avoided by staying on the seaward side of the ridge, to reach the summit of North Goatfell, 2,659ft (818m). Bear left and cross the mass of boulders to meet an exposed step with loose eroded granite. Negotiate this carefully to reach the crest of the ridge. Pass a buttress with more rotten granite, and continue to descend on a worn path; firstly on grass, then on a bouldery slope. A heathery shoulder follows with a tremendous view of Cir Mhor ahead, and descend easily to reach The Saddle. From this area covered with grit and gravel bear left and descend down a clear path through boulders, and then through boulders and heather. The path follows the river down the valley, sometimes wandering away and then rejoining it at an attractive waterfall, pool and birch trees. Always look back and admire the wonderful view at the head of the glen. Cross over a footbridge and follow the twisting track as it gradually descends to reach a gate. Pass a wood on the right to meet another gate. The Glen Rosa campsite lies down to the left, as the track becomes a lane to meet The String road. Turn left and walk for a short distance to the main road. Keep left, cross over Rosa Bridge and turn left through a lodge gate. The road is lined with beech hedges, which tend to obscure the three standing stones, two to the left and one to the right. The road bears right across a bridge in a wooded area, and passes the large house known as The Kennels. Just ahead, the waymarked Goatfell track crosses the road. Turn right and follow the track back to the car park.

WALK 4: Circular Walk Corrie, Coire Lan, North Goatfell, Goatfell, Meall Breac, Corrie
MAP: OS Explorer Sheet No: 361
DISTANCE: 6miles (9.6km).

Leave the south end of Corrie, near the Corrieburn Bridge, by the suggested way to Goatfell. The route follows the line of the Corrie Burn, passing through two deer fences, and heading straight on into Coire Lan. Note the Meall Breac rising on the left. The path then climbs steeply to reach the cairn on the ridge. Bear left up to the summit of North Goatfell, 2,659ft (818m). Continue along the Stacach ridge, avoiding the rocky tors by staying on the seaward side of the ridge. Climb up to the bouldery summit of Goatfell, 2,866ft (874m), complete with survey pillar and view indicator.

Leave the summit, and follow the ridge path in an easterly direction to reach an outcrop of rock. Aim to the left or to the right of the outcrop. The descent is still bouldery underfoot, and the path is braided in parts, before reaching the more level shoulder of Meall Breac. Keep straight on, where the Brodick path turns off to the right along a broad and boulder strewn crest. As the path skirts round the shoulder of Meall Breac, descend the heathery slope down to meet the Corrie Burn. Ford the steam, where there should be no problem unless the burn is in spate. Bear right down to a step stile in a tall deer fence. Continue to descend over a rough bouldery path to reach another deer fence with a gate. The path aims downhill between afforestation to join a clear track. Bear left to pass a small covered reservoir, and walk down the narrow tarmac road, back to the starting point.

WALK 5: Glen Sannox
MAP: OS Explorer Sheet No: 361
DISTANCE: 6.5miles (10.4km).

Glen Sannox is a beautiful valley that leads into the heart of the mountains. This is a pleasant walk that follows the Sannox Burn on a good path through heathery surroundings. Extensive sections of the path have been improved, including culverts and stone paving. Leave the car park at Sannox Bay, and walk up the lane past an old graveyard to the site of the former barytes mine. Evidence of the scattered tips remain at the site. Walk to the right and cross the footbridge over the north side of the burn. Alternatively, the Sannox Burn can easily be paddled across at times of low water. There is a splendid all-round view, which includes Cioch na h'Oighe, Cir Mhor, Caisteal Abhail and Suidhe Fhearghas. On reaching the head of the glen, the route rises steeply towards the cliffs below the Saddle. Ahead, there is a scramble over rock slabs, and a final steep and loose rock chimney up to the ridge cairn. Return by the same route.

Note: experienced walkers may descend from the Saddle and continue down Glen Rosa to reach Rosa Bridge (as Walk 3). Ensure that transport or pick-up has been arranged. Distance: Linear Walk, Sannox Bay – Rosa Bridge 8.25miles (13.2km).

Glencloy Water to Goatfell.

Goatfell.

Glen Sannox.

CORRIE AND SANNOX

Amongst the 14 villages on the island, the communities of **Corrie** and **Sannox** lie on the coast road to the north of Brodick. Corrie is a charming little seaside spot, it has a row of neat, colour-washed dwellings with attractive dormer windows nestling beneath the cliffs and close to the shore. An irregular group of cottages that form High Corrie, are situated on top of the raised beach.

The evidence of early settlement in the area points to a Neolithic chambered cairn near The Rocking Stone at **South Sannox**. There are Iron Age remains with the fort, An Cnap, at Mid Sannox, and a vitrified fort at North Glen Sannox. Also, there are Bronze Age standing stones near to Sannox House, and beside the Congregational Church in Sannox.

At the beginning of the nineteenth century, a time of demands for improved farming methods, the changes by the landowners meant that farms were divided into smaller units. This made it necessary for local people to look elsewhere for a living. However, white sandstone was being quarried at Corrie, and later, good quality red sandstone from a quarry behind the terrace of houses. This provided much needed employment, as the white stone was used in the construction of the Crinan Canal; and the red standstone was much in demand on the mainland. Another interesting industry here was the quarrying of limestone, forming caves in the hillside above Corrie. The mining of barytes was first carried out in Glen Sannox in 1840, and by 1862 some 5,000 tons had been produced.

The mine was closed by the 11th Duke of Hamilton, because he felt that it spoiled the beauty of the landscape. It was reopened after World War I, when a tramway and pier were built. By 1934, the output had risen to 9,000 tons, but the veins had petered out in 1938. After World War II, the mineral track and pier were demolished.

At the entrance to South Glen Sannox is a burial site shared by both communities. In a corner of the cemetery are the remains of St Michael's Chapel. Amongst the stones in the graveyard, is the grave of Edwin Rose, murdered in Upper Glen Sannox in 1889. John Watson

19

Laurie was convicted and narrowly avoided execution.

The Congregational Church at Sannox was built in 1822, and it is interesting to note that emigrants to Canada built a similar church at their new home in Megantic County. Corrie Parish Church, a fine red sandstone building, was built in 1886.

Halfway between Sannox and Corrie is a huge granite erratic boulder almost encroaching on the road. Named the Cat Stone on the map, it appears to be derived from clach a'chatha, which means – stone of the battle. There is a tradition of an attack by islanders on a Cromwellian foraging party near the site of the stone.

Corrie and Sannox welcome visitors and hope they will take part in the Corrie Capers. This is a week of events in the first part of August. Developed in 1981, it includes parades, shows, sports and displays for the entertainment of visitors; and ends with the burning of a symbolic longboat on Sannox beach, followed by bonfire and fireworks. Features and facilities in Corrie include: a village hall, harbours, car park and toilets, Free Church of Scotland, High Corrie Bunk House, stores, post office, cycle hire, Corrie Hotel, Corrie Crafts and pony trekking at North Sannox.

At **North Sannox**, a short stretch of road goes down to a most delightful picnic spot by the sea, NS015466. Visitors can walk to Fallen Rocks and Millstone Point, and return to the picnic site.

NORTH WEST ARRAN

Sections of the island's roads were constructed at various times in the nineteenth century. The route from Sannox to Lochranza across the Boguillie, 669ft (204m), was built in 1843. Up to that point, most traffic reaching Lochranza came from the sea, as there were only rough tracks over the pass. Even when the main road was built, it was a narrow road, and there were fords rather than bridges.

LOCHRANZA

The A841 climbs steadily from Mid Sannox to reach the top of the low pass, the Boguillie. It then descends down Glen Chalmadale beneath the steep slopes of Torr Head. The road flattens out, passing the Arran Distillery, and runs along the strand by the river and by the side of Loch Ranza. The charming village of **Lochranza** is spread along the shore on both sides of the loch, and was once one of the main herring fishing centres on the west coast of Scotland. The inner harbour is now used by pleasure craft that come in for shelter when there is a strong wind blowing from the west.

The ruined thirteenth- or fourteenth-century castle, situated on the gravel spit, stands guard over the entrance to the loch. It was at one time thought to be a tower-house, but is now believed to have been a hall-house, which was similar to an English fortified manor house. The clues included a blocked up doorway and a number of long arrow slits. The building was heightened in the sixteenth century, by one of the Montgomeries, to become a tower-house with internal modifications and the main entrance sited on the south-west wall. The Montgomeries were created Earls of Eglinton in 1507, and the castle remained in the family until it passed to the Hamiltons in 1705.

The Vikings knew the sheltered water of **Loch Ranza**, and established their homesteads in Glen Chalmadale. The land was cleared of stones and pastoral activities carried out. The safe harbour in the loch enabled them to explore the waters and nearby islands, and to exploit the rich harvest of the sea.

Herring mystery

In more recent times, Lochranza became a busy herring port. The silver shoals of herring have always remained a mystery. At the height of the fishing operations, no one could understand why the shoals were so numerous. However, one day they were there, and the next occasion they were gone. For season after season they had come into the Firth of Clyde, Kilbrannan Sound and Loch Fyne. Then suddenly they no longer came.

The fishing industry brought wealth and property to Lochranza. New homes were built, old properties renovated and farms and crofts improved. Men had to look further afield, but they used their sailing skills to become Master Mariners, officers, engineers in the Merchant Navy, and skilled at trades associated with shipbuilding.

Then the beauty of the island landscape began to attract the visitors, and the village catered for them; houses were let and for boarding accommodation, a new hotel was built – this is now the Youth Hostel.

Lochranza and the north end of the island, remained with its runrig system (communal farming) way of life, until the late nineteenth century clearances by the Hamiltons for sheep farming. Malcolm MacMillan was born at the Cock Farm in 1735, and lived on a number of communal farms in the area. He was the grandfather of Daniel, the founder of the publishing firm (1813–1857), and the great-great-great-grandfather of the Rt Hon. Harold MacMillan.

Steamers used to call at Lochranza, with the *Duchess of Hamilton* the last boat to call on the long journey from Gourock to Campbeltown. Nowadays, Caledonian MacBrayne run a summer ferry service across Kilbrannan Sound to Claonig in Kintyre, which takes 30 minutes. In winter, the ferry service runs to Tarbert in Kintyre, and takes 85 minutes. There is a memorial on the slipway at Lochranza to the 37 men of the submarine *HMS Vandal*, which sank in 1943, one and a half miles north-west of the village.

Facilities for visitors include a 9-hole golf course and putting green, tennis courts, a caravan and camping site, and possibilities for many good walks in the area. There is an excellent youth hostel that has comfortable self-catering accommodation for up to 64 people, with small rooms available for family use.

Lochranza.

WALK 6: The Cock of Arran, Laggan and Glen Chalmadale
MAP: OS Explorer Sheet No: 361
DISTANCE: 7½ miles (12km) Circular Walk

At the eastern end of Lochranza, take the signposted lane opposite St Bride's Church. Walk past the golf course, and turn left along the shore road to meet a row of houses. Continue on the track passing other cottages and along the raised shoreline at Newton Point. Just ahead, at map reference NR934518 is a location of interest to all geologists. James Hutton, who became a noted geologist, discovered older beds of schist overlain by younger sandstone. It proved his theory that layers of rock could become worn down, then covered with fresh rock strata.

Walk along the shingle shore to meet a challenging section of fallen boulders – watch where you are putting your feet! You will then pass a large sandstone block called the Cock of Arran. Eventually, the way becomes easier; note the eroded sandstone and the igneous dykes. Walk along the grassy foreshore to meet a boggy and rocky section. At this point the route passes through a small former industrial area, where poor quality coal was one mined to fuel the salt pans. Millstones were also manufactured at this location. At Laggan cottage, turn inland and ascend the hillside veering to the right along the grassy track; with the old intake boundaries and the remains of Cock Farm below to your right. The track gradually veers to the left and ascends to the highest point, Bearradh Tom a'Muidhe, at 862ft (263m). Looking back, there are fine views to Cowal and Bute; to the south the fine mountains of the Goatfell group are visible. Descend gradually, on a track that can be wet and muddy, and pass some cottages in Glen Chalmadale. Turn left on to the lane past the golf course and back to the starting point.

WALK 7: Gleann Easan Biorach, Loch na Davie, Gleann Diomhan and Glen Catacol
MAP: OS Explorer Sheet No: 361
Distance: Distillery, Lochranza to Catacol, 7½ miles (12km)

This is a walk through mountain glens, with splendid moorland scenery. The route is often wet and boggy in places, and there are many waterfalls to admire. A map and compass are essential. Walk alongside the Arran Distillery near the Ballarie Bridge, and climb up through the gap between An Stucan and Torr Head. The path emerges from the mini gorge to follow the steam into the moorland heart of Gleann Easan Biorach. There are many small waterfalls to admire on this section of the route before reaching the tiny Loch na Davie. This moorland lochan lies at the watershed between Carn Mor and Beinn Bhreac. Ahead, the serrated peaks of A'Chir, Beinn Farsuinn and Beinn Nuis appear on the skyline.

The path begins to veer to the right, and ascends round the shoulder of Beinn Bhreac to reach a cairn at the head of Gleann Diomhan. Descend the path into the glen, keeping the burn on the left. Further ahead, the burn rushes through a rocky chasm with attractive waterfalls. The bouldery path reaches an area enclosed by deer fencing. This is the Gleann Diomhan National Nature Reserve, home of two rare varieties of rowans (*sorbus*) – the whitebeam and the service tree. There is access to the trees by means of a ladder stile in the deer fence. Follow the path down to the narrow gorge where the trees cling precariously to its rocky walls.

Return to the main path and continue down Gleann Diomhan. After joining the path from neighbouring Glen Catacol the way underfoot becomes easier. The route closely follows the burn, then passes fields, to meet a stile in a fence. Aim for a clump of trees beside a bridge, and on to the main road. Turn right and walk into Catacol. In order to return to the starting point at the Distillery, Lochranza, there is a 2½ mile (4km) walk back along the hard surface of the A841. Attractive scenery though it is, it would be preferable at the end of the day, to have checked on the bus times, or to have made arrangements to be picked up.

The Isle of Arran whisky distillery was officially opened by the Queen in 1997. It is situated by Ballarie Bridge at the east end of the village. The home of Arran malt, it uses water cleansed by the granite as it comes down from the hills. Visitors can enjoy a dram at the end of the distillery tour, which is fully guided with an audiovisual presentation. There is an exhibition, a shop and a restaurant.

The history of Lochranza is very much associated with its isolation at the north end of the island. The surrounding mountains and lack of roads meant that most communication was by the sea. In the eighteenth and well into the nineteenth century, only rough tracks linked the crofts and farms usually above the raised beaches. Nevertheless, by the end of the nineteenth century, all the main roads in Arran had been built but they were only nine feet wide; two carts were just able to pass each other. The rugged terrain, landslips along the northern shore, and the presence of the Craw Brae, meant that wheeled transport by road was impossible from Lochranza and Catacol south.

WEST COAST TO AUCHAGALLON

From Coillemore Point the main road hugs the coastline very closely down the west coast of the island to Machrie Bay. The attractive row of cottages at **Catacol**, the Twelve Apostles, line the side of the road. They were built during the time of the 11th Duke of Hamilton, and were not completed until the middle of the 1860s. The dwellings were intended for the inhabitants of the old clachan at the head of the Abhainn Bheag burn, who were displaced by the late clearances in the north of the island. These particular clearances were to make way for deer not sheep. However, the people would not live in them, and it took some time before they were occupied by tenants.

WALKS IN NORTH-WEST ARRAN

WALK 8: Coire Fhionn Lochan
MAP: OS Explorer Sheet No: 361
DISTANCE: 3¼ miles (5.2km)

From Mid-Thundergay a signposted path points the way to Coire Lochan. Beyond the buildings of the settlement, pass through a kissing gate into open ground and proceed to an access gate through the deer fence. Cross over a small burn by stepping stones and bear right to join a second stream. In parts, the route is boggy as it crosses and recrosses the burn. Keep alongside the southern bank as it cascades over ledges of rock. Soon the bouldery path reaches two cairns, and looking back there is a splendid panorama of Kilbrannan Sound and the Kintyre peninsular.

The Fhionn Lochan lies in a deep hollow, a typical glacial corrie surrounded by the enclosing shoulders of Meall Bhig and Meall Biorach. Given good weather conditions, this is an idyllic spot with a good deal of atmosphere, where the crystal-clear water is edged by beaches of coarse granitic sand. Return to Thundergay by the same route.

NOTE: Keen hill walkers can extend this walk by climbing the pass between Meall Bhig and the ridge, east and south of Fhionn Lochan. Follow the broad shoulder and a boulder field to reach the cairn at 2,142ft (653m) at the head of Coirein Lochain. Continue round the top of the corrie to Meall Donn 1,923ft (586m) and on to the summit cairn of Meall Biorach, 1,808ft (551m). There are some steep sections of the path on the descent. Head for the western end of Fhionn Lochan and the return path to the starting point at Mid Thundergay. Total distance including this extension of the walk is 5½ miles (8.8km).

In this excellent walking area, there are other opportunities for tougher days on the hills. The above walk can be further extended by taking in Beinn Bhreac, Mullach Buidhe and Beinn Bharrain, with a descent to Pirnmill.

The wandering west coast road passes through small coastal settlements like Thundergay (guy) and Pirnmill. In between these places are the names of clachan communities such as; Lennimore, Auchamore, Penrioch, Altgobhlach, Whitefarland, Imacher and Balliekine, which are mostly situated above the coastal road. The clachan of Balliekine was the last community on the island to operate the ancient runrig agricultural system. It is of interest to note, that in many of the clachan communities, the crofters' meagre income was supplemented by illicit distilling in secret stills in the hills.

The village of **Pirnmill** takes its name from the former water-powered mill on the banks of the Allt Gobhlach. It used to manufacture wooden pirns, or bobbins, between 1780 and 1840, for the thread trade of Clarks (latterly) Coats of Paisley. Pirnmill was also a centre of a flourishing herring fishing industry, from the end of the nineteenth century until the end of World War II. Prior to the improvement of the roads, inter-settlement travelling was by sea. The steamers used to anchor off Pirnmill, and a large rowing boat was used to ferry passengers, luggage and even calves to the jetty. In the mid-nineteenth century, the fashion for deer stalking and grouse shooting by the landed gentry began. By the end of that century, after the island had been restocked with deer, **Dougarie Lodge** was built as a shooting lodge near the mouth of the Iorsa Water.

Once over the Iorsa Water, the land becomes lower in relief, as one passes into the farming area of Machrie, Shiskine and Blackwaterfoot. The fields are now a mixture of improved grassland and arable land, bordered by low hills, with slopes planted by the Forestry Commission. The Machrie Water enters the sea near the golf course, at the junction with the little road that is a link to the B880, the String. Along a track close to this turning is the late Neolithic or early Bronze Age Auchagallon Cairn, NR 893346. Although described as a stone circle, it is more likely to be a cairn. The site consists of a low mound of stones, surrounded by an intermittent ring of boulders, of which five larger stones are set close to the track on the west side. The little road continues past Machrie Farm to meet the String road, which climbs high over the central watershed to Brodick. If you have mail to post, look for an impressive red sandstone pillar housing a small red letterbox.

SOUTH WEST ARRAN

The immediate area was well favoured for settlement by early humans, and there is evidence of their occupation in the form of chambered cairns, stone circles, hut circles and standing stones. A little further south, a sign directs the visitor to the **Machrie Moor** stone circles NR 9032, opposite a small car park. The area contains a fascinating collection of Neolithic and Bronze Age monuments, probably the most remarkable archaeological site on the island. All the principal monuments lie close to the track leading to Moss Farm.

Pirnmill.

Machrie, standing stone.

Approaching from the west, the first monument has the disturbed remains of a large round cairn. Most likely Bronze Age, it is surrounded by an impressive boulder kerb. Continuing eastwards, on either side of the track, are hut circles and a standing stone. Further away southwards, are the locations of two chambered cairns and several hut circles. Close to the first gate, marked by a lone tree, are the depleted remains of a chambered cairn. As the track bends northwards, there is a stone circle with two concentric rings; both circles composed of small rounded boulders. Straight ahead for a short distance, is a small stone circle consisting of four low granite boulders. Excavations in 1861 revealed a cist containing a bronze pin, flints and a food vessel.

East of the farm buildings are a number of stone circles. From the north there is a circle with the remains of three stones just above ground level. The next site is particularly impressive, with three upright stones standing to a height of 18ft (5.5m); originally there were six or seven stones. Two cists were discovered here, containing a crouched burial, a food vessel and a cremation. There are two further stone circles; one that probably contained a ring of twelve tall sandstone slabs, and another with ten stones just above ground level. Here, it was discovered that there were post holes for an earlier ring of timber uprights.

South of the Moss Farm track, the A841 bends inland in order to avoid the high ground of Torr Righ Mor, before returning to the mouth of the Black Water. The village of Blackwaterfoot was the small port for the nearby communities of Torbeg, Ballymichael and Shiskine. The latter place takes its name from a corruption of the Gaelic for a marshy place. This area of small settlements was a hub of industry until the 1930s, with crafts and varied trades to fulfil the needs of the local population. After World War I, the large farms of Balnacoole and Shedog were divided into smallholdings.

According to tradition, Christianity was brought to other parts of Arran by St Molas from his lonely retreat on Holy Island in about the sixth century. There is a tradition that the Saint's last resting place was in the Clauchen Glen near Shiskine. The ruins beside the burial ground in Clauchen Glen are those of a church built in 1805, on the site of an earlier church. The church continued in use until 1889, when the new church dedicated to St Molas was opened. It is a distinctive red sandstone building, with a monumental effigy built into the west wall. The figure, now known to represent a medieval ecclesiastic, was taken from the church at Clauchen.

BLACKWATERFOOT TO CORRIECRAVIE

The tiny port of **Blackwaterfoot** was a busy centre, as most goods were brought in by smacks and puffers. This was gradually succeeded by lorry transport from Brodick. At one time a sailing packet boat operated between Blackwaterfoot and Campbeltown, and towards the end of the nineteenth century the settlement began to develop as the main tourist centre in the district. Between the two World Wars, more accommodation became available in hotels and guesthouses. Importantly, the **Kinloch Hotel** now has splendid facilities; such as, a heated indoor swimming pool, sauna, solarium and squash court. To the north-west of the village is a 12-hole scenic golf course, overlooked by the spectacular cliffs of the Doon, and bordered by a long sandy beach. Blackwaterfoot has other accommodation, shops, an all-year-round bowling green, tennis courts and a putting green.

To the south of Drumadoon Bay a signposted track leaves the road to the Neolithic/Bronze Age site at **Kilpatrick**, NR 906262. Originally, it was thought to be an early form of Christian monastery, or cashel. The remains comprise a large enclosure surrounded by an earth and stone bank. Archaeologists are undecided as to the interpretation of the site. However, it has been suggested that it was a late Neolithic chambered cairn, reused in the Bronze Age.

WALKS IN SOUTH WEST ARRAN

WALK 9: King's Cave, Drumadoon
MAP: OS Explorer Sheet No: 361
DISTANCE: 4¹/₂ miles (6.4km)

North of Blackwaterfoot, the coastline swings out to Drumadoon Point with a fine golden strand in between. A walk to the King's Cave, NR 884309 makes an interesting outing. Head north-west along the shore for half a mile, and follow a grassy path which passes two rocky outcrops. Beyond a stile, ascend towards the rock pinnacle, and continue northwards along the foot of the impressive columnar cliffs of The Doon to reach a wide grassy raised beach. The way climbs through sandstone outcrops to reach the King's Cave. It was reputed to be the hiding place of Robert the Bruce before he returned to the mainland. The legendary story of the spider is also associated with his stay in this isolated spot. The cave contains some ancient, though now faint, rock symbols, thought to date back to early Christian or Viking times. There are, in fact, two adjacent caves, of which the northerly branch is the important one. Near the inner end, on the rock face, is a large cross in the form of a broadsword. Further inspection will reveal the outline of a deer, a serpent, a man on horseback and a figure with outstretched arms. There are also some "ogham" inscriptions in the cave; these involve a code of letters represented by a combination of short horizontal and diagonal notches. These are cut along either side of one corner of a slab of stone.

A return can be made up the steep path that climbs to the top of the cliffs, round the east side of The Doon and on to the summit of the Iron Age fort. Further on, continue along the perimeter of the golf course back to Blackwaterfoot.

Beyond **Brown Head**, the main road climbs away from the coast, and links the settlements of Sliddery, Lagg, Kilmory, Shannochie, West and East Bennan. The road crosses the two major streams flowing swiftly southwards from their moorland and forested recesses in south Arran. The southern coastline is a magnet for geographers and geologists, who come to study the extensive sections of raised beaches. Above the cliffs are the remains of duns and chambered cairns. The shoreline is an interesting mixture of rock dykes, boulders, caves, slabs, shingle and sand. Along the quiet Corriecravie strand, visitors should take the opportunity of walking by the sea to enjoy the wonderful variety of summer wild flowers, and to view curlews, black-headed gulls, eider ducks, shags, cormorants, wheatears, whinchats and stone-chats. You are also quite likely to spot seals just offshore.

KILMORY TO KILDONAN

Just past Corriecravie, a track leads directly south of the road, to Torr a'Chaisteil dun, NR 922233. This Iron Age fort is typical of many hundreds of similar duns to be found in western Scotland. It consists of a rampart wall enclosing a circular mound about 46ft (14m) in diameter, with an entry on the east side. The road descends to **Lagg**, sheltered by a garland of trees, with the Kilmory Water alongside the gardens of the attractive eighteenth-century coaching inn. Close by the hotel, there is a post office and tearoom, and other places of interest are the **Torrylin Creamery** and the Island Porcelain building.

At this point, there is a lane to the left that runs along and then downhill to Kilmory Church.

The name **Kilmory** is derived from the Gaelic – Killmhuir, i.e. St Mary's. In 1711, Duchess Anne presented a second pair of communion cups to the church, as the first set had been destroyed in a fire. In the graveyard, the head-stones record many generations of local farmers, fishermen and sailors. In 1908, the schooner *Bessie Arnold* was wrecked on the rocks in a blizzard. All perished except the mate, and the ship's figurehead, that once marked the crew's grave, is now safely kept inside the church. The manse of Kilmory is an interesting and historical building, having been built around 1690. Part of the old structure remains, and it is the oldest inhabited manse in Scotland.

At the church, a sign points to the **Kilmory Workshop** at Cloined, where woodwork and pottery crafts may be of interest to visitors. Continue over the bridge and up the track to the workshop. Cars can be taken, and a small car park is available.

A Free Church was built and stands today at **Bennicarrigan** at the junction of the A841 and the scenic Ross Road. This route follows the valley of the Sliddery Water, climbing to a height of 935ft (285m) in wooded surroundings, before descending the Monamore Glen to Lamlash.

For the adventurous visitor, an expedition to the Carn Ban chambered cairn can be undertaken. Although there are various forest ways that may be used to reach the site, the most straightforward route is along the signed track from the main road, just east of Kilmory. (see walk 10)

Carn Ban, 4,000 – 3,000 BC

This Neolithic chambered cairn is located on sloping ground at a height of 902ft (275m) above sea level, MR991262. Due to its remote position, the cairn has been well preserved from plundering by stone robbers. It measures about 18ft (30m) by 59ft (18m) and its greatest height is 14.7ft (4.5m). At the north-east end there is a semi-circular forecourt flanked by two square-ended projections. At the centre of the forecourt, the entrance to the burial chamber is marked by two portal stones. One of the roof lintels to the chamber can still be seen. The chamber was divided into four parts, each separated by a stone slab. Towards the centre of the south-west end of the mound are several stones which probably indicate a second burial chamber. This could mean that the original cairn was enlarged to accommodate later burials. The only finds made after nineteenth-century investigations were a fragment of flint and a piece of Arran pitchstone. The acid nature of the soil had eaten away the skeletal remains, except for a piece of a long bone.

At Lagg, just beyond the bridge, a track gives access to Torrylin chambered cairn, NR955211. This cairn had a rectangular mound containing at least four compartments. On investigation the mound was found to contain human skulls and other animal and human remains. Grave goods consisted of a fragment of a neolithic bowl and a flint knife. East Bennan Chambered Tomb, 4,000 example of a four-sided and horned long cairn. It has been extensively robbed of stone, but the burial chamber is one of the longest in the Arran neolithic cairns.

Beyond the two cairns lies the sea, and although much of the immediate coastline is secluded and rocky, the longest and loveliest stretch of sand on the island is to be found here. East of **Bennan Head**, with its conspicuous quartz-porphyry cliffs, a loop road drops down to the sea at **Kildonan**. This name is derived from St Donan, an Irish monk, who lived in a cell or cill there in the sixth century AD. The "kil" prefix in a place-name usually indicates an early Christian monastic site.

There are opportunities here for exploring the rocky strand as far as the Black Cave. The front at Kildonan is a pleasant spot with sandy sections between the rocky dykes running out to sea. It is a lovely location for children, and there are sub-aqua facilities, self-drive cruise charter and boats for hire. At the end of the village are the ivy-covered ruins of **Kildonan Castle**. Only a fragment of walling remains, standing on the cliff top overlooking the sea. Although little

Kildonan.

WALKS IN SOUTH ARRAN

WALK 10: Auchareoch and Carn Ban Chambered Cairn
MAP: OS Explorer Sheet No: 361
Distance: From MR 970214 and return: 8½ miles (13.6km)
From Lagg, 10½ miles (16.8km)

NOTE: Even though the route is signposted, don't forget your map and compass. From Map Reference, NR 970214, leave the A841, and take the track which is also a designated off-road cycle route. The way passes through fields, then alongside afforestation, and on through a mixture of woodland and heather moorland. The track descends to a burn with the isolated farm of Auchareoch on the left. Proceed to a track junction, when signs point to Kilmory and Whiting Bay/Lamlash. Bear left for Carn Ban, cross a burn and continue to a sign for Carn Ban. Turn right along the forest ride parallel to the Allt an t'Sluice burn, and walk ahead to reach another sign indicating left. This forest ride is wet and muddy in places before arriving at a notice describing some details about the monument. After the visit, return to the starting point by the same route.

is known of its owners, or when it was built, it was probably a tower-house. The stronghold was given to John, the bastard son of Robert III in 1406. Later, it was a Stewart property, and records state that in 1549 the building was in the possession of James Stewart, Sheriff of Bute. Out to sea is the small tear-shaped island of **Pladda**, nesting place of common and arctic terns. It is only 27 acres (11ha) in area and was granted to the Hamiltons. The lighthouse was rebuilt by Stevenson in the 1820s and was manned until the 1980s. Although the island is small, it is interesting to note that it has its own fresh water supply. In the distance, to the right of the island, is the cone-shaped mass of Ailsa Craig.

SOUTH EAST ARRAN

From **Kildonan**, the minor road climbs up to meet the main road at Dippen, and continues high above Dippen Head. On the descent at Mayfield Farm, the A841 bends to negotiate the cliffs of An Garradh. There is a parking area just below; a good vantage point for splendid views beyond **Largybeg Point** across the Firth of Clyde to the Ayrshire Coast. The main road continues its descent to Largymore and crosses the Glenashdale Burn at Ashdale Bridge at the southern end of Whiting Bay.

The district has been inhabited since ancient times, with its chambered tombs of the Giants' Graves in forest clearings south of Glenashdale Burn, NS043247.

Smuggling and the running of illicit stills were profitable sidelines in the eighteenth century and outwitting the excise men added spice to a hard life.

WHITING BAY

Through the nineteenth century as the Clyde resorts became more and more popular, steamers brought day-trippers and tourists from Glasgow to **Whiting Bay**. The resort grew, with the provision of accommodation for these visitors. Boarding houses were built, hotels enlarged and amenities improved. There was no pier so passengers, luggage and freight were landed in small boars at the jetty and also at Kingscross. Later, in 1901, a pier was built at Whiting Bay and it held the record as the longest in the Clyde. However, due to rising costs and the increasing use of road transport, the pier was dismantled in 1964. The golf course was enlarged to 18 holes, tennis courts and a bowling green and a putting green were established.

At the present time, the **Whiting Bay Golf Club** hosts a number of events such as the Men's Open, the Ladies Open, Mixed Fours and a Junior Open. During the year there are many programme items, with a Fiddlers Concert, Jazz Café, Fun Day, Family Dances and the Hall Fête. On the north side of the resort is a sandy bay at Sandbraes. At the south end, by the Glenash-dale Burn, the Youth Hostel is now closed to individual members. For further details contact the Scottish Youth Hostels Association at 7, Glebe Crescent, Stirling FK8 2JA ☎ 0870 1553255.

WALKS IN SOUTH-EAST ARRAN

WALK 11: Giants' Graves and Glenashdale Falls
MAP: OS Explorer Sheet No: 361
Distance: (Including Giants' Graves) 3³/₄ miles (6km)

The walk starts from Ashdale Bridge at the southern end of Whiting Bay. Follow the narrow lane alongside the burn into mixed woodland to meet a junction of paths. Take the one on the left and climb steeply through woodland to reach a forest clearing. The Giants' Graves, NS043247, lie at 426ft (130m) above sea level. The material of the first Neolithic chambered tomb has largely gone, and the side slabs of the gallery have subsided inwards; but the horns can be traced. The second cairn is small and roughly oval shape with a single chamber.

Return the same way and descend to the path junction. Bear left with the way signposted to Glenashdale Falls. Continue through mixed woodland along a path that is muddy in places. Note the varieties of trees, such as conifers, birch, ash and alder as well as the noise of rushing water. A path descends to a viewing platform where the water cascades over quartz-dolerite sills in the rocky gorge. Return to the main path and climb to reach a wooden bridge across the gently flowing burn. Proceed along the path, through a gap in the stone dyke and take the right fork signposted to Whiting Bay. A little way ahead there are the scattered remains of an Iron Age Fort. The route continues to another waterfall viewpoint, then heads on to meet a forest road. Continue along this forest track to leave the woodland, as it descends to a minor road at South Kiscadale. Walk straight ahead and back to Whiting Bay.

At the north end of the resort, the A841 turns slightly inland to avoid Kingscross Point, where there are remains of a Viking burial mound and Iron Age Fort, NS056283. It is also a good vantage point for lovely views of Holy Island, with its classical shape, columnar cliffs and lighthouse.

LAMLASH

The coastal resort of **Lamlash** is situated at the head of a large bay, sheltered by the steep bulk of Holy Island. It is the administrative, health and education centre for the island. The bay is dominated by Holy Island, formerly eilean Molaise, named after the Irish Saint (Mo) Las. He lived as a hermit in a cave on the island, before becoming Abbot of Leithglinn in Leinster. Interesting relics have been found in and around his shelter. It was in Lamlash Bay in 1263, that King Haakon assembled a great fleet of galleys prior to the Battle of Largs. After the subsequent storms and defeat, the remnants of the Viking Fleet gathered before their final departure. In the twelfth century, Somerled established his dominion over Holy Island. In 1830 Holy Island became its official name when the village across the bay adopted the name of Lamlash;

corrupted through Elmolaise and Lemolash.

Lamlash was the embarkation point for Arran families; twelve families mainly from Sannox, 86 people. They left in 1829, having been cleared from their land to make way for agricultural improvements. The mound on the village green is said to be the spot on which their minister preached his final sermon. In front of Hamilton Terrace, is a rock monument erected in 1977 by descendants of those who left for Megantic County, 50 miles (81km) south of Quebec in Canada.

Potatoes

A notable son of Lamlash was Donald McKelvie, the 'potato king', who grew seed potatoes. He produced over thirty different varieties, all with the prefix 'Arran' in their name, such as Arran Banner, Arran Pilot.

The bay was a naval base, and before the 1914-1918 war, visits of the Fleet were social occasions. In World War II, Winston Churchill visited the bay, where there was a naval gunnery school and landing craft training.

The present parish church of Kilbride was built by the twelfth Duke of Hamilton in 1884. It has a number of beautiful stained glass memorial windows, a carillon of nine bells and a fine two manual organ. The spire of the former United Free Church is a conspicuous landmark, but the building is no longer used for church services. The ruined church of St Brigid in the Kilbride burial ground of Lamlash, was built in the fourteenth century, but was damaged by fire during the English raid of 1406. The chapel walls and graveyard contain sculptured stones, the oldest dated 1603.

At **Monamore Bridge**, there was once a water-powered meal mill on the site of the Paterson Arran Fine Foods outlet. The factory shop sells

Lamlash.

WALKS IN SOUTH-EAST ARRAN

Walk 12: Holy Island
MAP: OS Explorer Sheet No: 361
Distance: 4½ miles (7.2km)

A path rises from the jetty, and heads through the fields to the left of the Centre. It continues to climb beyond a wall through bracken, in a section where young trees have been planted. Follow the way markers as the path swings to the right, and cross at a stile to continue uphill. Higher up the impressive cone of Ailsa Craig comes into view. The clear path climbs more steeply in an area of heather, boulders and rock outcrops, to reach the subsidiary summit, Mullach Beag, 807ft (246m). From this point there are fine views around Lamlash and Whiting Bay.

From Mullach Beag, descend to a saddle and ascend steeply. Here, some scrambling is involved, although there are plenty of good holds for hands and feet to reach the summit of Mullach Mor, 1030ft (314m). In surroundings of heather, bilberry and rock outcrops, there are outstanding views of the island; across to southern Arran towards the northern peaks; along the Clyde to Bute and the Cumbraes; and south to Ailsa Craig. Descend steeply and negotiate some awkward sections of rock steps and broken rock. Take note of the warning about a number of dangerous fissures, and keep strictly to the path.

On reaching the shore path, bear left to the square-shaped Pillar Rock lighthouse at the south-east corner of the island. Retrace one's steps, and walk towards the other lighthouse. Look out for the cabin used by the Venerable Lama on the hillside to the right. Ahead, besides cottages and a walled garden, stands a row of small stones that display Buddhist inscriptions. Continue on the grassy path along the western shoreline of the island to pass more splendid rock paintings of Buddhist saints. As the north shore turns round a bay, the going is a little more rugged. Keep a watch out for steps that rise to a cave. This is the Saint's Cave, St Molas or Molaise, NS059297; it contains runic and Christian inscriptions, and there is a spring of fresh water close by. Return to the shore path, and then follow it round White Point back to the starting point at the jetty.

Note: Access to Holy Island is by a ferry service from Lamlash (Old Pier), hourly from Easter to the end of August. The journey takes 10 minutes. For further information, ☎ 01770 600998. For accommodation on Holy Island, ☎ 013873 73232. www.holyisland.org

preserves, mustards, chutneys and gifts. They operate a full catering range and are suppliers to hotels.

Today, Lamlash relies on farming and tourism. It is a centre for water sports of all kinds; yachting, marine and sub-aqua facilities. There is a marine store at the Old Pier, chandlery, fishing tackle, diving equipment, clothing and nautical books. The resort has the usual craft shops, including Studio 4 a jewellery workshop and gallery, and leather goods.

Facilities for visitors include tearooms, an 18-hole golf course with magnificent views of Holy Island, tennis courts, bowling green, putting green, cycle hire, sea angling trips; and there is safe bathing. Lamlash Gala Week offers various events, including the Urie Loch Race. For walkers with an adventurous nature, there is a rugged excursion from Monamore Glen through woodland to Urie Loch, lying in a moorland hollow at 1,329ft (405m). There are usually many species of birds around its shores.

HOLY ISLAND
(GAELIC – EILEAN MOLAISE; MO LAS' ISLAND)

Once part of the estate of the Duke of Hamilton, the island was bought in 1991 by a group of Scottish Buddhists; the Samyé Ling Buddhist Centre based at Eskdalemuir in Dumfries and Galloway. It was purchased on the understanding that the archaeological and spiritual amenities, flora and fauna would be protected. The Buddhist Order intends to develop the island as a spiritual sanctuary. The Peace Centre has been established in the original farmhouse building. There are accommodation facilities, as well as a library, meeting hall and dining room. Also, there is an information centre and tearoom. Springs supply the fresh water, which is heated by solar panels.

All visitors are asked to abide by the rules of Buddhism: protecting life, speaking the truth, respecting other people and their property, not indulging in sexual misconduct and refraining from tobacco, alcohol and drugs.

The massive bulk of Holy Island is thought to have been formed from an invading ring of riebeckite-trachyte, a fine-grained micro granite, similar in composition to Ailsa Craig; that was forced up through the New Red Sandstone sedimentary rocks. The highest points on the island are; Mullach Mor, 1030ft (314km) and Mullach Beg, 807ft (246m).

The island is a nature reserve where many trees once grew. Since the Buddhist community arrived here, many thousands of trees of varying species have been planted by volunteers. Wild goats roam over the rocky slopes, together with a number of Soay sheep. Peregrine falcons breed on the cliffs, eider duck nest on the shores and there are gulls, cormorants, guillemots and curlew.

There are three aims of the Holy Island Project: to develop a Retreat Centre at the south end of the island, to establish a centre for Peace and Reconciliation in the north part, and to promote a conservation element involving bracken control and tree planting.

RETURN TO BRODICK

From the north end of Lamlash, the A841 turns sharply inland. At the brow of the hill there is an undulating stretch of road and a sign that indicates a forest car park. It is a very pleasant spot, with picnic tables set out in clearings amongst the trees. Across the road, a Forestry Commission sign indicates the details of ways to Brodick and Lamlash. A four-mile walk, there and back, can be undertaken to Dun Fionn. Then, by following the clear path along a forest ride, and bearing left up a wide forest clearing, the route turns right along the heathery ridge of the Clauchland Hills to the cairn at 853ft (260m). The next stage is to follow the up and down course of the path, gradually descending to the edge of the forest to meet a gate and stile. There are choices of routes that could be followed here; by turning left to Corriegills and Brodick, turning right to Clauchlands Farm and Lamlash, or straight on to the Iron Age hill fort of Dun Fionn 538ft (164m). The fort is conspicuous with its rounded summit and survey pillar. It is a wonderful viewpoint, looking south-east to Holy Island, and north to Brodick Bay and its superb backcloth of jagged peaks.

From the picnic area, follow the main road as it descends through the afforestation to emerge for its short journey to Brodick Bay and the pier head.

3. Isle of Bute

The Isle of Bute is one of seven islands in the Firth of Clyde. In the north, the landlocked waters contain a wide variety of long peninsulas, deep-cut bays, fiord-like lochs and narrow straits or kyles. The latter geographical feature has the distance separating one piece of land to the next down to just a few yards. This location is at the north end of Bute, where cattle used to be swum across the kyle to Colintraive and on to markets in central Scotland.

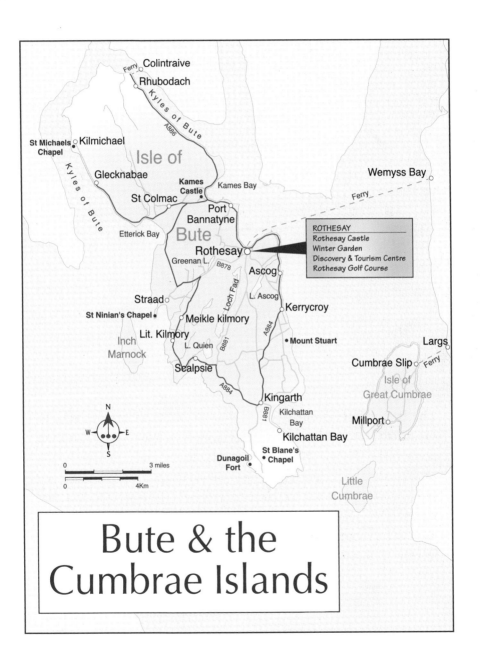

Ferry Colintraive
Rhubodach

Kyles of Bute
A886

St Michaels Chapel · Kilmichael

Kyles of Bute

Isle of

Glecknabae

Kames Castle · Kames Bay

St Colmac

Wemyss Bay

Ferry

Port Bannatyne

Etterick Bay

Bute

Rothesay

Greenan L. · B878

Ascog

ROTHESAY
Rothesay Castle
Winter Garden
Discovery & Tourism Centre
Rothesay Golf Course

Straad

St Ninian's Chapel ·

Meikle kilmory

Lit. Kilmory

L. Quien · B881

L. Ascog

Kerrycroy

A884

· Mount Stuart

Largs

Loch Fad

Inch Marnock

Scalpsie

A884

Cumbrae Slip · Ferry

Isle of Great Cumbrae

Kingarth

B881

Kilchattan Bay

Millport

Kilchattan Bay

N
W · E
S

0 ____ 3 miles
0 ____ 4Km

Dunagoil Fort

St Blane's · Chapel

Little Cumbrae

Bute & the Cumbrae Islands

Bute is about 15½ miles (24.8km) long, and varies in width from 1¼ to 5¼ miles (2–8km). To the east lies the Clyde coast of North Ayrshire and Renfrewshire; to the south east are the islands of Great Cumbrae and Little Cumbrae; northwards are the narrow Kyle of Bute and Loch Striven, and northwest the Kilfinan peninsular and Loch Fyne. To the south-west stands the mass of the Isle of Arran and its impressive granite peaks.

Before the reorganisation of local government in 1974, the County of Bute consisted of Arran, Bute, the Cumbraes and three smaller islands. Nowadays, the islands are part of the wide-ranging region of Strathclyde, and come under different administrative districts: Ailsa Craig – Kyle and Carrick; Arran, Holy Island and the Cumbraes – North Ayrshire; Bute and Inchmarnock – Argyll and Bute. At the height of its popularity, Bute was an attractive destination for thousands of industrial workers going 'doon the watter' during the Glasgow holiday fortnight. Today, it is within commuting distance from Glasgow.

It is not easy to determine the meaning of the island's name, and from which source the name has been derived. In Gaelic, the town of Rothesay was always *Baile Bhoid*, possibly meaning 'the settlement of the corn island'. Another explanation is that the name, Bute, harks back to the Pictish inhabitants of the island. However, its name may stem from its contact with the Vikings. To the Norsemen it was known as; Rothirs – ay, or Rudri's – ay; Rothir's or Rudri's island, from a character mentioned in Haakon's Saga. So, that in Norse times, Rothesay was the name of the island, and not the town itself.

HERRINGS

From the point of view of fishing, it would appear that the first settlers in Bute used tidal fish traps. Remains of one of these constructions have been discovered on the west coast of Bute north of Ettrick Bay, just south of Clate Point. Here a row of large stones parallel to the shore had in-turned ends. These traps were usually baited with shell fish. There is some belief that the position of the fish traps were in relation to the sites of deserted homesteads, pointing to a crofting, fishing and farming way of life.

In 1764, the Earl of Bute began to implement a programme to develop the island's natural resources. Indeed, the following year saw the establishment of a Custom House Station, which was quickly followed by the granting of a herring fishing licence. It was recorded that in 1799, the herring were so plentiful around the coast of Bute that 50,000 barrels of fish were taken by the boats. This amount of fishing activity meant that the quay and harbour at Rothesay were rebuilt and enlarged and became the centre for the herring trade.

The herring catch reached its peak around the 1850s, which ran parallel with the heyday of the Clyde fishing fleet. The great shoals of herring in the waters around the island, and particularly in Loch Fyne, became legendary. For over

100 years the herring was salted and sold, not only for home consumption, but to countries abroad including Germany and Russia.

The decline in the Loch Fyne herring industry started about the early 1900s, but the communities that served the herring fleet also enjoyed the golden age of water transport at that time. This was the distinct period of the steamers who brought the tourists in vast numbers on day trips and cruises along the Firth of Clyde. Along Loch Fyneside, small settlements enjoyed this prosperity, and there were at least seven piers, and other places where a boat came out to meet the steamer. Overall, in the area of the Firth of Clyde, the great fishing and holiday boom led to the expansion of resorts such as Largs, Millport and Rothesay. The piers became great meeting places, when from early morning until evening, a continuous number of small steamers called. In the summer of 1913, it was recorded that these little steamers made over 100 calls at Rothesay, their decks crowded with passengers.

Then suddenly, the herring was no longer there, and this mystery has never been solved. However, a likely answer to their disappearance was the lack of a close season, as the boats fished day in, day out, throughout the year. The fishermen of Bute switched to the catching of white fish, but gradually throughout the 1950s to the 1970s, the decline continued in the fish stocks of the Firth of Clyde.

Look out for Local Kippers: they are superb!

THE PUFFERS

Another feature of the time between 1900 and 1920 was the Puffer: a small steam lighter. Puffers were frequently used as general cargo carriers along the coastal waters of western Scotland. There were three types used; for canal work, in estuaries, and for off-shore journeys. The famous puffer epitomised as the *Vital Spark*, was featured in Neil Munro's tales of Para Handy, with his crew of Dougie, Macphail, Sunny Jim and The Tar.

The quality of the herring fishing and its sudden disappearance was often a source of conversation and discussion between Para Handy and the crew of the *Vital Spark*.

"Of aal the fish there iss in the sea," said Para Handy, "nothing bates the herrin': it's a providence they're plentiful and them so cheap!"

"They're no' in Loch Fyne, wherever they are," said Dougie sadly.

"I wouldn't say but you're right," agreeably remarked the Captain. "The herrin' iss a great, great mystery. The more you will be catchin' of them the more there iss; and when they're no' in't at aal they're no' there" – a great philosophical truth which the crew smoked over in silence for a few minutes.

"The herrin' wass that thick in Loch Fyne in them days," recalled the Captain, "that you sometimes couldna get your anchor to the ground, and the quality was chust sublime. It wassna a tred at aal so much as an amusement."

The stories about Para Handy and the *Vital Spark* give a clear picture of the way of life, and places visited, around the Firth of Clyde. The tales were first published in 1955, and are still available in paperback format. The 2004 edition contains 18 previously uncollected stories.

LANDSCAPE

The island's attractive and varied landscape has been created by its underlying geology. Afforestation nestles closely to heather-covered hills, and mixed woodland lines the edges of sheltered freshwater lochs. Arable and pasture land meet the curving stretches of sandy bays. Along the island's lonely northern coastline, the stony Maids of Bute keep watch across the Kyle. The island can be divided into three sections, the northern part, the central part and the southern part.

THE NORTHERN PART

This area close to Argyll is mainly composed of Highland quartzites, with a southern rim of Highland schists. Then south of the lower lying area of deposited material between Kames Bay and Ettrick, there is another band of schists. This is followed by another mass of quartzites ending at the junction with the Highland Boundary Fault. The hard rocks of the north form rolling hill country, bare heathery moorland and rock outcrops. A large part of the north-eastern side is covered with afforestation. The Highland quartzites are hard rocks, and they have created rolling hill country, bare heathery moorland and rocky outcrops. The area is drained by the Glenmore and Ettrick Burns, and

rises to the highest point, Windy Hill, at 912ft (278m) about sea level.

South of Kames Bay and Ettrick Bay, the land is lower in altitude, with enclosed arable and pasture land, and with farmsteads dotted around the fringe. There are some occasional rock outcrops and these become more obvious in the area around Loch Dhu, where a series of small craggy summits dominate the scene; such as Craw Hill, 463ft (141m) and Barone Hill, 531ft (162m).

THE CENTRAL PART

The Highland Boundary Fault greatly influences this area, which has resulted in the valley containing the large freshwater Loch Fad and the smaller Loch Quien. At the north end is the wide sweep of Rothesay Bay, and the valley runs south-westerly to Scalpsie Bay. South of the Highland Boundary Fault, the underlying Old Red Sandstone rocks have created a landscape of gentler scenery. There is a band of mixed woodland on the north edge of Loch Fad and around Mount Stuart House, as well as other tracts of conifer plantations. The areas in between are a rich and fertile mixture of arable and lush pastureland. Continuing southwards, there is another lower level neck of land composed of deposited material stretching from Kilchattan Bay to Stravannan Bay.

THE SOUTHERN PART

This is the tail of the island, which has a scenic surprise in store. Here, apart form two small sections of Old Red Sandstone the majority of the area consists of carboniferous

Rothesay harbour.

Rothesay castle.

Rothesay has been a holiday resort for over 150 years. The height of its popularity as a holiday centre, and the Firth of Clyde as a sailing area, was reached in the 1870s; and the years from 1900 to 1910 and up to World War I. The life of the island changed to a different pattern after the passing of the cotton mills and the demise of the fishing fleets. Bute, and in particular Rothesay, took on a new role as a tourist centre, as the fashion for residential holidays brought thousands of visitors to the Clyde coast. Between the two World Wars there were periods of prosperity and recession, but World War II affected Bute greatly. There were many evacuees, a Commando training base on Inchmarnock island and a naval centre at Rothesay. After World War II, there were again periods of decline and change, with holiday makers taking advantage of new leisure opportunities, such as cheap foreign package tours.

At the present time, much emphasis is being devoted to the promotion of Bute as an unexplored island. It offers activity holidays; sporting possibilities: walking, angling, pony trekking, cycling and sailing; journeys to places of historical and archaeological interest; studies of the local geology and natural history; and an appreciation of beautiful coastal and landscape scenery.

The shoreline is always full of interesting attractions for children, and there are safe sandy bays and quiet beaches. The island is conveniently sheltered from the worst of the weather by neighbouring Arran and the Kintyre Peninsular, but all prospective explorers should have waterproofs, stout footwear and carry a good map, preferably, OS Explorer 362, Cowal West and Isle of Bute.

Rothesay has a number of excellent visitor attractions, namely: Rothesay Castle, Bute Museum, Public Library, the Discovery Centre and Leisure Pool. Outside the town, there are the Ardencraig Gardens, the Ascog Hall Fernery and Garden, and the magnificent Victorian Gothic mansion of Mount Stuart House, standing in 300 acres of glorious landscaped gardens.

There are two riding centres on the island that give advice to both novice and experienced riders. There are quiet lanes, woodland tracks and wide sandy beaches. For those who like to feel the pull of a large brown or rainbow trout, then Bute offers wonderful opportunities for angling. Loch Fad and Loch Quien, in particular, are noted for their large trout; Loch Ascog for pike and Greenan Loch for tench, roach and carp.

Although Bute is a small compact island, it is scenically varied enough to interest both walkers and cyclists. There are quiet roads with leafy hedgerows and excellent vantage points – don't forget the tearoom at Ettrick Bay! For walkers, there are low hills, quiet lanes, tracks and coastal paths with fine views out to sea. There are a variety of shorter walks; as well as the waymarked 30 mile (48km) long distance path, the West Island Way, that traverses the island from south to north.

The Isle of Bute Discovery Centre is housed in the fully restored Winter Garden. The Tourist Information staff can provide an excellent range of books, maps and leaflets for visitors to the island.

Panoramic views are par for the three golf courses on the Isle of Bute. Rothesay has an 18-hole course; Port Bannatyne with its 13-hole course, with par 67 based on 13 plus five holes, and Kingarth set by the shore has a 9-hole course. The sheltered waters of Rothesay Bay are ideal for watersports, such as windsurfing, dinghy sailing, water or jet skiing; for enthusiasts with their own equipment. The waters around Bute are excellent for sailing, when an experienced yachtsman can hire a yacht, or otherwise bring their own craft. Also, there are five-day RYA sailing courses for all levels of experience.

Bus services run from Rothesay to Port Bannatyne, Ettrick Bay, Rhubodach and Kilchattan Bay on schooldays only; and on non-schooldays, Saturdays and Sundays, from Rothesay to Kilchattan Bay, Port Bannatyne and Ettrick Bay. Services also run to Ascog Hall and Mount Stuart House, and there are local bus routes around Rothesay itself. Everyone is welcome aboard the *PS Waverley*, the last sea-going paddle steamer in the world. Cruises run from Rothesay along the Clyde Coast, Easter weekend and June to August.

volcanic lava flows, similar in relief to that of neighbouring Little Cumbrae Island. It is a lovely, green landscape of bracken (turning gold in autumn), and grass-covered escarpments, prominent outcrops and mini glens. The ridges and summits afford panoramic views of the Cumbraes and the mainland to the east, and towards the jagged profile of Arran's northern peaks. There are also good scenic prospects of Bute northwards to the Cowal peninsular. The highest points of the escarpment ridges are; Suidhe Chatain, 515ft (157m) and Torr Mór 489ft (149m).

ROTHESAY

The residents of **Rothesay** are proud to be able to acknowledge the fact that they live in a Royal Burgh. The charter was granted on 12 January 1400 by Robert III of Scotland, at the royal castle. This gave protection to the merchants of Rothesay, by allowing them a monopoly of all trade into and out of the town.

ROTHESAY CASTLE

The early history of **Rothesay Castle** is unclear. It is thought that the date of the original structure is in the latter part of the twelfth century. Norway ruled the Western Isles until the Treaty of Perth in 1266 gave the lands back to Scotland. But prior to that event, many of the island territories had broken away from Norse rule; and to combat this weakening in their hold over the islands, the Norse king, Magnus Barefoot, led several expeditions to the Hebrides to reassert Norse control. It was possible that Magnus was responsible for erecting the fortress; but what is certain is that the castle of Rothesay became a Scottish royal castle.

The stronghold was besieged and captured by the Norsemen in 1230, with the attackers having to withstand volumes of molten lead and pitch before overcoming the defenders. It was captured again in 1263 during King Haakon's campaign, prior to the Battle of Largs. The four imposing drum towers seem to have been added in the thirteenth or early fourteenth

Splendid convenience

On disembarking from the ferry at Rothesay Pier, one should not walk past the Victorian gents toilet, even if the immediate need doesn't arise. This splendid Victorian edifice, commissioned in 1899, was completely restored and officially opened in 1994. Originally only for men, a section was added for ladies when it was being refurbished. Never will the call of nature be answered in such opulent surroundings. The interior decor is absolutely magnificent – green marble splendour, decorative white ceramic tiles, ceramic mosaic floor, glass-sided cisterns and gleaming copper pipes; and each urinal stall imprinted with the title, the 'Adamant', indubitably, a top of the range product from Twyfords in Staffordshire. There is an interesting notice which states that visitors, especially female visitors, are offered the opportunity to view the gents at the following times: 10.00am, 1.00pm and 4.00pm.

The Rothesay Discovery Centre.

century. Work was carried out on the enclosing walls, and the moat was reshaped to provide room for the towers. The redoubtable gatehouse was begun in the reign of James IV, who granted the hereditary keepership to Ninian Stewart in 1498; the gatehouse was completed by James V in 1541. The interior of the castle contains a chapel dedicated to St Michael.

The castle was restored between 1872 and 1879 by John Crichton Stuart, 3rd Marquess of Bute. The hereditary keeper of Rothesay Castle still remains in the Stuart family. The building was formally placed in the guardianship of the State in 1951. The Duke of Rothesay is Prince Charles.

MUSEUM AND LIBRARY

Situated in Stuart Street, the **Museum** was built in 1927 by its patron, the 4th Marquess of Bute, for the Buteshire Natural History Society. It is a delightful building with an attractive outside appearance. The Museum is the main source of information about the Isle of Bute, and houses important records of Bute's natural, archaeological, geological and industrial history. There are extensive displays of birds and island wildlife, and exhibits from every period of Bute's history form early stone tools to Clyde steamers. Look for the Bronze Age jet (lignite) necklace found in a burial site on the island of Inchmarnock.

There are fascinating details here about Bute's contribution to, and association with, HM Forces during World War II, particularly the importance of submarine, midget submarine and human torpedo training. Children are well catered for; with special displays, including a touch table, toddler's case and aquarium. A museum quiz is available free of charge. Copies of informative booklets produced by the Buteshire Natural History Society may be purchased here. They deal with Rothesay and outlying parts of the Isle of Bute.

Also situated in Stuart Street, the **Library** is part of the Moat Centre, a not so visually attractive building next door to the Museum. Some excellent archive material and rare books may be found here, that record the history of Bute. There are records of the Censuses of the island parishes (1841–81); old Parish Registers before 1855, and files from the island's newspaper, *The Buteman* – founded in 1855.

LEISURE BUILDINGS

The Victorian **Winter Garden** building is situated in the Esplanade Gardens near to the pier head. This Grade A listed structure built on to an existing bandstand in 1924, and now fully restored, is set amongst colourful flower beds. An integral part of Rothesay's history, this cast iron and glass building, complete with domed roof, houses the **Isle of Bute Discovery and Tourist Information Centre**. An interactive exhibition introduces visitors to the island's attractions, and includes fascinating film footage of past and present Bute. The centre also includes a genealogy section and a cinema/theatre. The Bistro has the benefit of sea views across Rothesay Bay.

Further along the esplanade

stands **Rothesay Pavilion**, a large hall representing the pre-war (1937) style of abstract design. Its well-appointed spaciousness is much in demand as a dance hall, concert venue, for a flower show or as a conference centre. An extensive restoration programme will be undertaken by Argyll and Bute Council.

THE HIGH STREET, ROTHESAY

If you come off the pier at Rothesay and walk straight inland, you meet the castle on the right. Near the corner of Castle Street and High Street is the old **Mansion House**, which was built in 1681 by George Cunningham, and once the town residence of the Marquesses of Bute. Continue straight ahead past the Leisure Pool and Public Park on the right and the Victoria Hospital on the left. A little beyond on the left wall is **St Mary's Well**. The church on the right, the old Parish Church of Rothesay, is the **High Kirk of St Mary and St Bruoc**. In the church grounds is the Chapel of St Mary, probably fourteenth century, which contains a medieval knight and grave slabs. Behind the church is the **House of Bute Mausoleum**, containing the ancestors of the present Marquess. Other burials of interest are Bishop Wallace, Stephanie Hortense Bonaparte and Robert Thom, the hydraulics engineer.

AROUND ROTHESAY

Close by is the **Bute Creamery**, a cheese making establishment, with a shop and visitor tours facility. The building beyond, on the edge of town, is the Primary School overlooking Loch Fad. The B881 road proceeds to descend gently through farming country, passing Lochs Fad and Quien on the right and Loch Ascog to the left. Ahead lies Scalpsie Bay, and in the distance the jagged peaks of the Isle of Arran form an exciting backcloth.

Returning to Rothesay the same way, at the brow of the hill near Crosseg, there are fine views ahead of Rothesay and the Cowal hills. Bear right just past the hospital, where the road bends left to meet a junction. Turn right and ascend through woodland and then keep left. Players at the 18-hole **Rothesay Golf Course** may find it difficult to address the ball properly, when there are such magnificent views over mountains, lochs and bays.

Continue past the camping and caravan site. Then bear left down the twists and turns of Serpentine Road to reach Trinity Church at the junction of Castle Street and Bishop Street. The castle lies straight ahead.

COTTON MANUFACTURING INDUSTRY

In the latter part of the eighteenth century, and part of the nineteenth century, an important cotton manufacturing industry was based at Rothesay. It lasted at least until 1860, and for a period of 60 years, up to fourteen per cent of the population worked in the cotton mills. The mills were dependent on an adequate water supply; so Robert Thom, a water engineer, planned a series of water-cuts and aqueducts to collect as much water as possible. He used the contours

Walk 1: Circular Walk – Bogany Wood, Rothesay
Map: OS Explorer 362 Cowal West and Isle of Bute
Distance: 2$\frac{1}{2}$ miles (4km)

Start from Rothesay Castle, walk along Castle Street to the foot of The Serpentine and turn left along Bishop Terrace. Watch out for a green signpost where the path leads on into woodland. Continue through Bogany Wood to reach Eastlands Road and turn right. Follow the road past the golf course and bear left down Serpentine Road. At this point an interesting diversion can be made; look out for the signs to the viewpoint of Canada Hill. Its name is said to have derived from the time when islanders left for Canada, and relatives and friends watched their boats sail away down the Firth of Clyde. Descend the Serpentine Road back to the starting point.

Walk 2: Circular Walk – Barone Hill, Rothesay
Map: OS Explorer 362 Cowal West and Isle of Bute
Distance: 3$\frac{1}{2}$ miles (5.6km)

From Rothesay Castle, walk up High Street to the High Kirk. Go through the churchyard, descend some steps and cross Mill Lade, then follow Thom's Lovers' Walk Cut to reach a minor road. Turn left, then right, into the field and accompany the wall to the corner of Craigberoch Wood. Aim for the ruined farm, and just before it in the field is a standing stone – look for the inscribed marks or 'cups' on the reverse side. Continue through a gap in the gorse keeping the farm on your right. Walk ahead, and turn sharp right down the track, to meet a gate on the left opposite Barone Hill. Descend down the field to a stile, and climb up to the summit of Barone Hill 531ft (162m). The top is a magnificent viewpoint, covering most of Bute, and the exciting skyline of Arran. The hill fort sited on the summit measures 200ft by 145ft (61m by 44m) within two now ruinous and plundered stone walls.
Descend from the hill by following a stone wall to a stile, and then left down to the water board road. Follow the road to a junction of four ways, and take the path to the causeway between Kirk Dam and Loch Fad. Pass Lochly Cottage and Ashfield Farm to meet the B881. Bear left and walk down the High Street back to the starting point.

Walk 3: West Island Way
Map: OS Explorer 362 Cowal West and Isle of Bute
Distance: 30 miles (48km)

This long distance path was opened in 2000, and traverses the Isle of Bute from south to north. It starts from Kilchattan Bay and finishes at Kames Bay, a distance of 30 miles (48km) of waymarked walking. The West Island Way offers a superb variety of landscape, from moorland, farmland, seashore and forest; it reveals many aspects of geography, geology, ruined and abandoned settlements and natural history. The grade of walking is relatively easy, with sections of coastal footpath, farm track, forest ways, minor lanes and roadside verges.

From Kilchattan Bay, the path follows the rugged coastline around Glencallum Bay; and then turns inland past Loch na Leighe to reach St Blane's Chapel, an early Christian Monastery founded in AD600. Continue past the ruined church to a gate, and follow the grass track gently uphill. Descend to a stream, and climb up to the shoulder of Suidhe Chatain. Descend alongside woodland towards Kilchattan Bay, and follow the track on the left beneath Suidhe Plantation. Cross the road, and walk towards Stravannan Bay alongside the golf course. Leave the shoreline and take the track to Langalbuinoch Farm; bear left for a short distance along the road, and take the track on the right by a copse of woodland to pass Upper Stravannan Cottages. The route turns left at the end of woodland to reach a junction. Turn right along the track named 'Lord James' Ride and proceed across Scoulag Moor (No, it isn't Siberia!). Turn left through a gate, and walk along the Moor Road; a track that descends to Loch Fad to bear right at the north end of the reservoir. Continue along the minor road to reach the B878 on the edge of Rothesay. Turn right, and then left across the fields to bear left at a school. Head along the minor road almost to Westlands, and go through a gate on the right, through the fields and two more gates. Aim left through the fields and two more gates. Aim left through a gate just prior to Gorans, and walk round the top side of the dwelling to meet Kames Hill Plantation.

Descend through the woods and keep above Port Bannatyne to reach the A844. Turn left and walk along the pavement with a view of Kames Castle. Further ahead, take the B875 and use the roadside verge to meet the farm road to Glenmore. Turn right, and walk past Lower Ettrick, Upper Ettrick and Kilbride to follow the valley of the Glenmore Burn. Pass Glenmore Farm, along the track and path, to an isolated group of trees at the ruined settlement of Achavoulig. From the gate, head down to the burn and cross by the big stone.

Aim in a north-west direction towards the middle of the afforestation; follow the forest track in a northerly direction for a distance of 1½ miles (2.4km) to reach Map Reference: NS01657350. At this point, the forest track bends sharply to the east. Follow the way down to meet another forest track coming in from the right, and bear left to meet the road at Rhubodach. Turn right and walk along the roadside verge by the Kyles of Bute to Ardmaleish. Then use the pavement to reach the finishing point at Kames Bay.

A footprint route map of The West Island Way may be obtained from the Tourist Information Centre at Rothesay.

of the ground to capture the flow of other streams. The enterprise was particularly successful as it raised the level of Loch Fad, and doubled the waterpower for the cotton mills. Remarkably, he carried out this work without the aid of Ordnance Survey maps, which were not published until fifty years later. At one time his enthusiasm went a little too far, because he cut off the water supply to Mount Stuart, the home of the Marquess of Bute. This led to a lengthy legal battle concerning the water taken from the Scoulag Burn.

Many of Thom's aqueducts are still in place today and marked on the Ordnance Survey Explorer Map of Bute; it is a fascinating business following the courses of these remarkable water cuts.

However, after only 10 years, there was only one mill remaining, and by 1882, the industry was virtually ended. There were various reasons for this decline in the cotton industry on Bute; a combination of factors, the need for heavy machinery in unsuitable buildings and geographical circumstances of transport and distribution.

BUTE TRAMWAYS

The Bute tramway system was a unique feature, being the only one of its kind on a Scottish island. A track was laid in 1882 between Rothesay, Guildford Square and Port Bannatyne for horse-drawn trams. The open-topped cars ran at 15-minute intervals, depending on the whims and natures of individual horses. At first the single track posed difficulties, but these problems were overcome by the installation of loop lines at certain places. The system was electrified in 1902, and extended to Ettrick Bay in 1905. This extension must have been a great joy for visitors as the track ran through open meadows.

However, the advent of the motor car, charabanc and motor bus radically changed the communication system on the island and, sadly, the final tram left Rothesay on 30 September 1936. The Bute Tramway left behind an impressive record of 54 years of service: 20 of horse-drawn trams and 34 under electrification.

NORTH BUTE

Travelling north from Rothesay the main road keeps to the shoreline to reach Ardbeg. The village is almost entirely residential and merges into **Port Bannatyne**. The road splits here, with the minor route keeping to the shore round Ardbeg Point and the A886 takes a more direct route. Wooded Kames Hill adds a leafy touch as it descends to meet the main road. The sea front contains a few services, shops, tearooms and public houses. The village is quiet now, but the pier was a busy centre during the heyday of the Clyde steamers; it was a regular port of call for sailings in the Kyles of Bute and Loch Fyne. The settlement developed quickly between 1890 and 1910, when many buildings were constructed, and efforts were made to promote the village as a holiday resort.

At the height of its prosperity, Port Bannatyne was an important link in the island's tramway system.

The tramcars met the crowds of visitors alighting from the steamers. Firstly, they took the horse trams, and later when the system was electrified, the new extension to Ettrick Bay. Port Bannatyne was well known throughout the area for its boatbuilding expertise in the construction of small fishing boats or skiffs. There was another boat-building yard just to the north at Ardmaleish.

Port Bannatyne takes its name from the Bannatyne family of Kames Castle. **Kames Bay** (Gaelic: camus, bay) is a peaceful deep-set indentation of Loch Striven, and almost opposite its meeting with the Kyles of Bute. These sheltered waters are particularly enjoyable for the yachting enthusiasts. There is good anchorage where seals may be watched and the surrounding scenery admired. As well as being a good mooring spot for yachts and other small craft, much larger ships have used its natural shelter.

Activity in wartime

During World War II, there were memorable happenings at Port Bannatyne, when battle-scarred ships were salvaged and repaired; notably the burned and shelled tanker *San Demetrio*. The waters of the Firth of Clyde during that time teemed with camouflaged warships, troopships and merchantmen.

Just inland from Kames Bay, near the junction of the A886 and the A844, stands the impressive tower house of **Kames Castle**. It is also attractively situated beneath the sheltering slopes of Edinbeg Hill. The earliest records refer to John, son of Gilbert around 1334; this building, the former seat of Bannatyne's, is one of the oldest continuously occupied houses in Scotland. The tower house is four storeys high with a crenellated parapet and a steeply pitched roof with crow-stepped gables. The strength of its walls is impressive too; they are 6ft (1.8m) thick and overall, the building measures 36ft by 26ft (11m by 8m). For extra defence it was originally surrounded by a moat, but only traces remain. The western side is now enclosed by later farm and estate buildings. Note: The estate is private property, and the house is NOT open to the public. Also within the estate is **Wester Kames Castle** built in the sixteenth century, once completely ruinous and now restored. This tiny former fortified building measures only 25ft by 21ft (7.6m by 6.4m).

NORTH TO RHUBODACH

From Kames Bay it is 3³/₄ miles (9.2km) to the ferry slipway at Rhubodach. From the north end of the bay, the road leaves the shoreline and crosses the flatter ground at Ardmaleish. After 1 mile (1.6km) it rejoins its pleasant scenic way, forestry on the flanks of Windy Hill on one side, and the waters of the Kyle on the other. **Rhubodach** (Gaelic – *Rudha – Mhodach*) is the end of the road. Across the Kyle at Colintraive the A886 continues to

Loch Fyneside and Strachur Bay.

From Rhubodach a track leads to **Balnakailly Bay**, and seasoned explorers can walk pathless to Bear Craig, and beyond round Buttock Point to visit the '**Maids of Bute**'.

In Neil Munro's Tales, Para Handy was asked to take a small boat across the Kyle to the 'Maids of Bute'. His task, on a beautiful day, was to paint the stones red and white. In his imagination they were two lovely girls; but in reality, he commented that they would be good enough for tourists!

ETTRICK BAY

From Rhubodach return to Kames Bay, and turn right on the A844 where a view can be obtained of Kames Castle. Continue along the main road, and then straight ahead on the B875. Just before Colmac Bridge is the ruinous **church of St Colmac**, built in 1836 by Lord Bute. Services in Gaelic were held there for many years, but eventually dwindling congregations forced its closure. Across the road, marked on the map as Cnoc on Rath, is an old ditched mound. Interestingly, throughout Antrim, there are many examples of circular rings called raths. Although they are often called ring forts, excavations have shown that they were essentially domestic in purpose.

On the slopes of Edinbeg Hill to the north are tips of slate waste from the former quarries. The workings go back to medieval times, but, since the 1820s, the small blue slates were thought to be impractical for large scale use. In the field near East St Colmac Farm stands a **carved stone cross**, which probably came from a Celtic chapel that once stood on the site. Further on, in a field on the left hand side of the road, stands the remains of a **Bronze Age stone circle** with some tall trees. Beyond lies the sea, and the curving stretch of golden sand called **Ettrick Bay**. At the present time there is an extra point of interest here, in the shape of a beached coastal vessel. Also, before you leave the beach, examine the basaltic trap dyke at low tide just west of the burn mouth. Near to the road is a parking area and toilet facilities. The **Ettrick Bay Tearoom** is open all day for snacks and light meals.

The road crosses Drumachloy Bridge and becomes narrower, as it continues round **Kildavanan Point** along the Kyles of Bute. It passes an old shoreline and cliffs near to Scarrel Point – the field is a good example of a raised beach. Continue for 1 mile (1.6km) to where a rough track climbs the hillside to the ruined farm of **Lenihall**. Opposite this point, on the shore, are the remains of one of the **old fishtraps** found around the shores of Bute. This consists of a line of boulders parallel to the shore line and turned in at the ends. The trap was baited with shellfish to attract fish at high tide. Nets or wicker barriers were used to trap the fish within the enclosure.

GLECKNABAE

The narrow tarmac road ends at **Glecknabae**, where there is limited car parking space. Nearby Glecknabae Farm offers tourist accommodation. In the field south of the farm, stands a **Neolithic chambered cairn**. On excavation, the burial cairn was

Kames Castle.

Ettrick Bay.

found to be standing on a Mesolithic midden, containing oyster, whelk and limpet shells. These remains date back to the time of hunter gatherers, people who were here before the Neolithic people. The cairn was originally constructed with three burial chambers separated by slabs inside the portal stones. It is likely that the cairn was used for burials into Bronze Age times. Pottery bowls with flattened rims have been recovered, together with pieces of pitchstone, bones and shards of pottery.

From the parking space, the farm track passes the South Wood of Lenihuline, where a signpost directs visitors to **Carn Ban chambered cairn**. A path ascends for a 20-minute walk through pleasant native oak woodland to reach the site. Although greatly plundered this Neolithic long cairn runs down the slope in the ground. It is about 180ft (55m) long and 30ft (9m) wide. There is a burial chamber at each end, but with no façade and another chamber near the east end. Return to the track to the point where the shore line begins to bend away to the west. In the first field on the left is the Neolithic chambered cairn of **Michael's Grave**. The chamber is practically all that remains in two parts, and the portal stones stand closely together.

Just beyond Kilmichael Cottage, a track on the right climbs up the hill to **Glenvoidean Neolithic burial cairn**. The chamber lies within a small cairn, with extra side chambers added later with porches and façades. The whole structure was enclosed in a roughly rectangular-shaped cairn, with an outer kerb marking the outline. It would appear that this burial site was used for hundreds of years according to the finds, and burials continued to be placed here by Bronze Age people. Evidence of burnt material and pots can be seen in the Bute Museum. All these ancient sites point to a farmed and populated coastal area of North Bute. Other evidence showed that this cairn was used as a corn drying site by medieval farmers. The stones were used, thus destroying a great deal of evidence. However, some green-glazed pottery was uncovered.

Descend to the farm track and walk towards Kilmichael Farm. Take the last gate on the left as far as the first gate on the left. Proceed across the field to the remains of **St Michael's Chapel**, which stand on a raised knoll. This small Christian building may possibly date back to the sixth century, although nothing of this period survives. The present chapel contains a stone altar and a recess in the wall, which possibly held church vessels. The graveyard contains some cast iron headstones from the 1890s.

When going back along the farm track to a point level with Michael's Grave, there is an opportunity to visit the remains of the old **Ferry House and Inn**. Follow the path round the top of the beach to the ruined house. It used to serve as a waiting room and inn for passengers travelling on the Blair's Ferry to a point just south of Kames. From the car park at Glecknabae return back along the road to Ettrick Bay.

WEST AND CENTRAL BUTE

From Ettrick Bay, there is a footpath that follows the edge of the shoreline, crosses St Colmac Burn to meet another parking area. The B875 road travels inland past the St Colmac Farms to meet the A844. Turning right, brings you back to the parking area at the south end of Ettrick Bay.

The road turns south leaving behind the lush pastoral surroundings, with a landscape of hedged fields gently rising to Creag na Buidsich, 482ft (147m). Here the upland pasture is a mixture of scrubland, bracken, heath and rough grassland. To the south of this rolling upland lies **Greenan Loch** and the B878 road back to Rothesay. The south-western slopes of this upland area have some rock outcrops before meeting the A844. A number of farms are spread out round the edges of this pastoral upland, and to the west, grassland and strips of afforestation shelve towards the sea. There are more farmsteads along the valley of the Greenan Burn as it flows towards **St Ninian's Bay**. At the bay's north end is the tiny settlement of **Straad**, and northwards there is a line of old sea cliffs, and the accompanying features of raised beaches.

Peaceful farming country it may be, but there is much evidence of past history on the ground and in the names of the farms. There are burial cists, small forts or duns, standing stones, sites of early homesteads and chapels, and the remains of a castle. These indications from the past may grip your imagination; they may spur you to explore Bute's ancient heritage and history, and to understand the customs and way of life of these early people.

There are early Christian sites, such as **St Ninian's Chapel**, which tell of the early missionary faith. Then there is the impact of raiders, colonists and settlers that often meant destruction and pillage; or at other times, the dawn of new cultures and skills.

Ancient names

Names of places, homesteads and farms give a fascinating insight into their beginnings and derivation from other cultures. The island has a wonderful mixture of Gaelic, Norse and English names, for example:

Largievrechten, (Gaelic), *Learg-a-bhreachdain* – the slope covered with wheat.

Straad, (Gaelic), *sraid* – a street.

Ardroscadale, (Gaelic), *ard*; (Norse), *ros* – both mean point; (Norse), *dalr* – dale.

Scalpsie, (Norse), *scalpr* – a small boat; (Gaelic), *aig* – bay.

Birgidale, (Norse), *borgr* – fort; *dalr* – dale or valley.

Barmore, (Old English), 'Cranberry moor'.

Milton, (Old English) – *middle Tun; mill Tun*.

Ladeside, (Old English) – water course.

At the point where the A844 executes a sharp right-angled bend at Ballianlay, take the minor road down to Straad. Nowadays, this tiny community has a village hall, a public telephone box, a few houses; and is also the starting point for a short walk of 2 miles (3.2km), there and back, to St Ninian's Chapel. Up to the end of the nineteenth century, Straad was a self-contained bustling settlement; it had a sheltered anchorage, a busy fleet of herring boats and a variety of craftsmen, such as a joiner, a blacksmith, a cooper and a miller. For their relaxation, there were two licensed inns in the locality. At one time the herring was smoked and all the villagers had a donkey in order to convey the kippers or fresh fish to Rothesay. Also, large quantities of cockles were raked from the sands of St Ninian's Bay, and were similarly carried to Rothesay to be sent on to Glasgow.

St. Ninian's Chapel

Approaching from Ballianlay, turn right at the hamlet and walk past the few houses; firstly on the road, and then on the track down to the shore of St Ninian's Bay. Proceed through the gate by the ancient standing stones, and walk ahead across the narrow shingle bank on to St Ninian's Point. Of this sixth- or seventh-century building, dedicated to St Ninian, the only remains are the foundations and part of the garth wall. It is possible that the chapel was abandoned, after the Viking raids, which ravaged so much of the western coastline of Scotland in the eighth or ninth centuries.

The original entrance may still be seen facing seawards and across to the mountains of Arran beyond. A little distance away is a small stone-lined well, only a few feet in diameter. Also, close by, are the masonry ruins of a fish processing building where the herring was smoked.

St. Ninian was a missionary, who was based at his religious centre at Whithorn on the Solway Coast. He sailed along the western seaboard of Scotland, even as far as the Shetland Isles; in order to spread the Christian faith, and to establish chapels like the one on St Ninian's Point.

On to Kilmory

The main road travels towards Rothesay, and then angles back sharply from its junction with the B878 to follow the course of the Greenan Burn. Both to the north and south of this junction there are locations that may well have associations with water mills in the past. Certainly, at **Greenan Mill** where the ruins can be seen, there was an inn until the 1870s. Below the road junction there is a dwelling by the burn called Milton, which means Mill Tun.

Ahead, a thin shelter belt of deciduous trees runs for $\frac{1}{2}$ mile (0.8km) on the west side of the main road. This strip of woodland indicates the position of the farm Meikle Kilmory, and the remains of **Kilmory Castle** situated besides the farm. This was the Crowner's Castle whose owners were entitled to dispense justice within the authority of their own territory. They had the summary power of arrest, charge and sentence over those people who broke the law. It is on record that a Norse raiding party attacked the castle in the same year as the Battle of Largs.

It will be noticed that the rising land behind the farm is in contrast to the ground on the seaward side. To the east, between the farm and the Highland Boundary Fault, is an area of metamorphic folded quartzites, with grits and grey blue slates. A series of craggy outcrops run north-east to south-west from Barone Hill to Tarmore Hill.

The ground consists of scrubland bracken, heather and rough grassland. To the west of Meikle Kilmory lush farmland, composed of the underlying deposited material, slopes gently to the sea.

In a remote spot between Kilmory Hill and Barmore Hill lies the **Bicker's Houses Chambered Cairn**. The burial chamber is the main feature of the plundered remains. It measures 15ft (4.5m) by 3^1/$_2$ft (1m) wide, and is divided into three compartments by two septal slabs. The large portal stones stand less than one metre apart with a septal slab immediately behind them. Interestingly, the word Bicker is Old Scandinavian, meaning the village marsh. The name probably poses more questions than answers. In the immediate area there is the crannog on Loch Quien with a causeway leading to it; probably Late Bronze Age or Early Iron Age, and the remains of another on Loch Dhu. Did Norse visitors find the chambered tomb and name it the burial site of people who once lived on the crannogs?

Just before the viewpoint on the A844 looking across the water to **Inchmarnock**, is the site of **Kilmory Chapel** between Little Kilmory and the sea and Bronze Age burial cists. On excavation, they were found to contain the bones of young children between the ages of seven and thirteen, according to subsequent research on their teeth. An urn recovered from this site is now in Bute Museum.

INCHMARNOCK

The island lies just under a mile, at its nearest part, off the west coast of Bute; it is 2^1/$_2$ miles (4km) long and ^{3}/$_4$ mile (1.2km) wide. St Marnock arrived on the island probably in the early seventh century and established a Christian chapel and a monastic community. Although there are few remains to be seen of the chapel, fragments of Celtic stone crosses have been recovered from the burial ground and walls. One cross shaft has three crosses carved on one side, and the shape of a cross or sword blade on the other. Another broken cross head from Inchmarnock is a reminder of a Christian symbol, from the time of the Viking raiders and colonists who came from Scandinavia to the Firth of Clyde. Inscribed on it in fragmentary runic writing is the following inscription; 'this cross was erected to Guthleif' or Guthleik. These items are now in Bute Museum.

During the eighteenth century, some of the church's stone was plundered by the farmer to build the nearby farmhouse, and a century later even gravestones were taken from the burial ground to build a byre.

Until fairly recent times, there were two working farms on the island; Northpark and Midpark. Although only separated from Bute by a narrow strip of water, the Firth has treacherous currents and is subject to sudden squalls. For example, during the winter months of the early seventies, the tenant of Midpark was only able to cross to Bute four times within a period of three months. There are no pier facilities, only landing places, suitable for a landing-craft type of vessel.

The island is now privately owned, and visiting yachtsmen and other intrepid visitors should try to obtain permission first before wandering about on shore. The geology of the island is similar to Bute and composed mainly of Highland quartzites and some areas of more recent deposits. Inchmarnock is a veritable nature reserve, exceptionally rich in wild flowers and dwarf hazel, rowan and birch trees. There is a prolific birdlife, with the island having the largest herring-gull colony on the Firth of Clyde.

In the extreme north of the island, the skeleton of a young woman was discovered in one of the stone burial cists, during the excavation of a Bronze Age cairn. Lying by her side was a 139 jet (lignite) bead necklace and a flint knife. The beads for the necklace have been restrung and are now proudly on show in Bute Museum in Rothesay.

During World War II, the inhabitants of Inchmarnock were evacuated, and the island was used for naval gunnery practice and as a commando training area. There was a considerable amount of damage, particularly to one of the farm buildings.

SCALPSIE BAY TO ROTHESAY

From the viewpoint at Mecknoch, the road continues to a parking area overlooking **Ardscalpsie Point** and **Scalpsie Bay**, with another vantage point on nearby Tarmore Hill. This lovely, peaceful area around the Point and the Bay has a number of interesting features to explore, including the small **Iron Age fort of Dun Scalpsie** and the **Haystack rock**. The former measures about 90ft (27m) by 80ft (24m) within a dry-stone wall, entrance on the north-west. The latter lies close to the northern shore of Scalpsie Bay and appears to be on the wrong side of the Boundary Fault. This rocky mound is composed of Old Red Sandstone breccia.

Descend the hill to Scalpsie Farm and cross over Ladeside Bridge, just south of Loch Quien. Turn left on to the B881 and enter the valley of the Highland Boundary Fault. This central valley runs towards Rothesay Bay, and contains **Loch Quien, Loch Fad and the Kirk Dam**. A little way to the north and south of the valley, in more elevated locations, are **Lochs Dhu and Ascog** respectively. The underlying geology has determined the nature of the soil, vegetation and surrounding landscape. There are metamorphic Highland quartzites with igneous rock to craggy outcrops and a terrain of heather and rough grassland. To the south of the valley, the underlying Old Red Sandstone has generally created good soils of a fine loam type. Both shores of Loch

Fad are well wooded particularly on its northern side.

Loch Fad, the long loch, is classified by Scottish Nature as a site of Special Scientific Interest. It is over 2 miles (3.2km) long, 1/4 mile (0.4km) wide and 36ft (11m) deep. This impressive water feature is noted for its scenic beauty, for its rich variety of wild fowl, and for its bird life. Ospreys have been occasional visitors, and there are goldfinches, yellow wagtails, yellow-hammers, long-tailed tits and woodpeckers.

Various fishing competitions are held on Loch Fad throughout the year, with rainbow and brown trout angling from boat or from the bank. There is fly-fishing from March to December; bait and spinning (bank only) from March to October. Loch Quien is a smaller loch set in more fertile surroundings. It is easily accessible and boats are available. There are shallow areas suitable for wading, with deeper water in the middle. There is fly fishing only for wild and stocked brown trout from March to October.

A short distance along the B878 from Rothesay, a minor road turns left at Barone Cottage for Loch Fad. At a triple junction, one path leads down to the causeway, and the middle road heads for **Woodend House**. This was built in 1825 as a quiet retreat for the famous Shakespearean actor Edmund Kean. The house has a lovely curved staircase and its windows look out over Loch Fad. Edmund Kean wished to escape the numerous incidences of scandal in London – wild living, adultery and performing in a drunken state. At the entrance to Woodend House are theatrical busts on pillars of the dramatist Massinger and Shakespeare on the left and the actors Kean and Garrick on the right. The pillars mark the end of public access on that road.

The softer land on the south side of Loch Fad, provides enjoyable excursions on the pleasant open moorland for walkers, cyclists and horse riders. From Rothesay, a track leaves the B881 and passes Lochend at the southern tip of Loch Ascog. The track proceeds across Scoulag Moor to the War Memorial on the A844 road. There are added bonuses on this excursion, with refreshments available at **New Farm**, and a circular ride or walk following **Lord James' Ride**.

Suitably refreshed, steps can be retraced over Scoulag Moor back to the B881. Follow the road down the valley heading south, and enjoy the company of those beautiful stretches of water, Loch Fad and Loch Quien.

SOUTH AND EAST BUTE

South of Loch Quien, and beyond its junction with the B881, the main road heads in to the southern part of Bute. To the west lie the small indentations of Gallachan Bay and Stravannan Bay. The A844 keeps roughly to an average height of 102ft (31m) above sea level, as it gently undulates towards the crossroads at Kingarth. Westwards, lush pastures slope very slightly to a fine length of old sea cliffs from Ambrismore to near Langalbuinoch, a distance of 1 3/4 miles (2.8km). These old cliffs, rising above an area of raised beaches, contain several caves and a small fort.

From Kilchattan Bay in the east to Stravannan Bay in the west, a neck of lower lying land of deposited material separates areas of higher land. Running north to south roughly down the middle is a windbreak of conifer plantations. To the west of the woodland there is a 9-hole golf course, a landing strip and standing stones.

To the west of the **Kingarth Hotel**, a minor road turns south, passing a group of standing stones in a clearing in **Blackpark Plantation**, the remains of a Bronze Age stone circle. The road bends sharply to negotiate Lubas Crag, with **Dunstrone Iron Age Fort** on a knoll above the sea. Just opposite Dunagoil Farm is a lay-by for access to the famous **Dunagoil Vitrified Iron Age Fort**. It will take about 20 minutes to reach the base of the crag, and care is needed whilst negotiating the craggy top.

DUNAGOIL FORT

Dun-na-ghoil (Gaelic) – the fort of the stranger, has been excavated several times. It occupies a narrow and rather abrupt cliff, which rises 100ft (30m) above the shore. There is a cave at the foot of the cliff, where many remains dating from Neolithic and Bronze Age times have been recovered. It has been suggested that the fort dates from 850BC, and the interest is centred on the vitrified nature of its defences. Here, in long stretches of its summit wall, the stones have been melted due to the application of tremendous heat. The glossy

appearance of the stones is probably the result of a high silica content. Research has shown that the stones were probably strengthened by timber supports, with timber buildings against the wall's interior side. Whether it was from enemy attack or by accident, the timber caught fire, and fanned by a strong coastal wind would cause high enough temperature to melt the stones.

The fort is defended partly by the steep flanks of the ridge and partly by the heavily vitrified wall. Two entrances, both reported to have been fitted with bar holes, gave access to the interior.

The site is also remarkable for the wealth of material recovered both from the fort and the cave. The cave at the foot of the cliff appeared to have been occupied for three hundred years. A considerable amount of Iron Age evidence was also recovered – pottery, a bloomery for smelting iron, clay crucibles for casting bronze, animal bones, ornaments made from bone and lignite, spinning whorls, querns, whetstones and pieces of flint. This evidence illustrates the thriving nature of this well-established community, manufacturing and trading a rich variety of goods.

Nearby, the site of **Little Dunagoil Fort** showed traces of an Iron Age rampart, as well as occupation from the Bronze Age until the thirteenth century. Many of the finds from both sites are on display in Bute Museum. Return to Dunagoil Farm and continue down The Plan road to a parking area, NS093531, above Garrochty Farm, for convenient access to **St Blane's Church**.

St. Blane's Church

From the parking area cross over to the gate, and ascend the gentle slope by following the hedgerow. Ahead, lying in a peaceful sylvan setting, on a grassy ledge surrounded by tall trees, stand the remains of St Blane's Church. It is not exactly known when Christianity arrived in Bute. The recovery of several carved crosses and the location of early chapel sites dedicated to saints like Ninian, Catan and Marnock prove the existence of an active Christian community by AD600.

Tradition records that St Catan founded the monastery here near Dunagoil, having fallen out with his sister who had become pregnant. The child born was Blane, who eventually returned to Bute and was united with his uncle. In time, Blane became abbot of the monastery and bishop of the surrounding area. After Blane's departure, Daniel was bishop about 659, Iolan in 689 and

Above: Looking towards Kintyre from Torr Mor.

Below: St. Blane's Church.

Abbot Ronan is recorded in 737.

However, before the end of the eighth century, the Norsemen were raiding the seaboards of northern Britain, and what happened to the monastery is unknown. It was presumably abandoned by the monks, and occupied by the Scandinavian raiders and colonists. During the nineteenth century, various items of Viking date were found here, including a hog-back tombstone.

The existing remains of the monastery show that the oval wall of the upper churchyard probably follows the boundary of Blane's early church. This wall was extended at a later date, when perhaps a second chapel was built to the south of the original church. The brothers probably used the upper churchyard for the burial of the monks, and the lower burial ground for lay people.

The land outside the inner cashel was a large area bordered by rocky cliffs to the west, and enclosed by a revetted earth bank on the other sides. Most probably, this boundary defined the land between the monastic area and the world outside. The inner sanctum contained the monastery buildings: the abbot's quarters, the individual cells of the monks, the refectory, a building for the novices, and a guesthouse for visitors. There would have been workshops, gardens and living quarters of the brothers.

The remains of some of these buildings can be seen at the base of the cliffs, together with a well. Also here is a large oval enclosure built with sizeable stones, and mysteriously known as the 'cauldron'; its date and function is quite unknown.

Just beyond, is a gate in the wall with a footpath signposted – the route of the West Island Way and also Walk 4 to Torr Mór and Kilchattan Bay.

KILCHATTAN BAY

From the parking areas follow the Plan Road to the main road, and bear right onto a detached section of the B881. Here Kingarth is one of the oldest recorded place-names in Bute. Today, the hotel provides restaurant and accommodation facilities. Continue down the road to reach the wide expanse of pink-coloured sand that forms **Kilchattan Bay**. Kilchattan takes its name from the early Christian saint Catan, who was thought to be the uncle of Blane.

Kilchattan's wide sandy bay and beautiful beach is a great favourite with holiday makers. However, until the 1840s it was a quiet backwater with a few fishing boats, and some employment in a small tileworks. But in the last quarter of the nineteenth century it was 'discovered' by the burgeoning Clyde tourist trade, and steamer services connected it to Wemyss Bay, Fairlie and Millport. It became a popular summer resort; a jetty was built, together with a hotel, houses and apartments, and an anchorage secured for small boats. Today, this is an attractive holiday location with fine sands and panoramic views along the Firth of Clyde and across to the Cumbraes; it is also a convenient base for touring and exploring the Isle of Bute.

For walkers, Kilchattan Bay is also the starting point for the West

Island Way (see walk 3). In fact, there are several interesting geological features in the neighbourhood. Following the coastal path to the south there are volcanic crags to see, and at **Hawk's Nib**, the remains of prehistoric fishes have been found. Continuing round the headland of Rubh'an Eun, there is the lighthouse on the edge of **Glencallum Bay**, and a stretch of remote indented coastline.

A shorter walk (distance: 2³/₄ miles [4.4 km]) from Kilchattan Bay takes in the ruin of **Kelspoke Castle**, Upper Reservoir, Hawk's Nib and a return back along the coastal path to the starting point

From Kingarth, a minor road, called the Bruchag Road, leaves the junction at Kingarth for a short journey close to the east coastline. It touches an area of quiet farming country, plantations and farmsteads, with good views out to sea, and through the extensive woodlands of the Mount Stuart Estate. Turn right on reaching the main road,

WALKS ON THE ISLE OF BUTE

Walk 4: Circular Walk St Blane's Church, Torr Mór, Kilchattan Bay, Largizean
Map: OS Explorer 362 Cowal West and Isle of Bute
Distance : 6¹/₂ miles (10.4 km)

Cars may be parked at the corner of the road leading to Garrochty Farm; map reference NS093531. Go through the gate opposite with a sign to St Blane's Church and follow the hedgerow up through the fields. As one climbs a little higher, look back to St Blane's Hill and Dunagoil Fort, and beyond to the mountain profile of the Isle of Arran and distant Kintyre. The ruins of the church stand in a beautiful setting beneath the bracken-covered ridge of Torr Mór. The site is sheltered by tall trees in peaceful surroundings. Tradition records that St Catan founded the monastery here in the late sixth century, and was succeeded by Blane, who became abbot and bishop of the surrounding area. In time, Blane moved eastward to found a church, which was later to become Dunblane Cathedral.

Proceed to a gate on the left of the site, footpath signposted, and gently ascend the track. At the top, bear right through grass and bracken to reach the ridge. Walk along the escarpment, taking in the two summits of Torr Mór, 489ft (149m) and 479ft (146m). From the ridge there is a wonderful panorama: south to the Firth of Clyde, east to the Great and Little Cumbrae, west to the Isle of Arran and north to the Kyles of Bute.

Walk back along the ridge and turn right. Follow the way marked route, descend to a stream, and climb up to the shoulder of Suidhe Chatain. Descend alongside woodland towards Kilchattan Bay, and bear left behind the houses. Follow the track beneath Suidhe Plantation to reach the road and turn left. Proceed along this quiet lane, the Plan Road, past Largizean Farm back to the starting point.

and proceed for 1½ miles (2.4 km) to **Kerrycroy Bridge** and the entrance to **Mount Stuart House**.

MOUNT STUART

The public are not likely to see a more breathtaking and romantic setting of a palatial home than the Victorian Gothic mansion of Mount Stuart. Already attracting up to 28,000 visitors a year, it has become a magnet for visitors to the Isle of Bute, and has greatly helped to influence the development of tourism on the island. Also, the importance of the grounds and gardens, which have seen a process of expansion and improvement since the first gardens were laid out in 1716, should not be forgotten.. Mount Stuart's 300 acres (122 hectares) now make a fascinating mixture of woodland, wilderness and designed landscape.

Family history

The present building is the second mansion to be built on the site, as the original central core of the house was destroyed by fire in 1877. Mount Stuart is the extravagant composition of the 3rd Marquess of Bute (1847–1900) and the imaginative skill of his architect Sir Robert Rowand Anderson (1834–1921). Rebuilding began in 1880, and it was ready for occupation in 1886. Great interest was generated at the time, when a heated swimming pool was installed, the first in any house. Also breaking new ground, was the fact that Mount Stuart was lit by electricity, the first in Scotland.

The Crichton-Stuart family, Marquesses of Bute, can trace their ancestry back to Anglo-Norman beginnings. Walter Fitz-Alan became Steward to King David I. It was from the office of Steward, from the word itself, that the surname of the Butes, Stuart, originated. The Crichton element was only added to the Bute's family name by the 2nd Marquess of Bute in 1805, when his mother Penelope Crichton was the heiress of the 6th Earl of Dumfries.

By 1204, the hereditary Stewards or Stuarts, held lands in Bute. One of their descendants, Walter married the daughter of Robert the Bruce, their son becoming the first Stuart King, Robert II. He married twice and fathered thirteen children and eight out of wedlock; so it is difficult to trace which one of these children is the ancestor of the Stuarts of Bute. However, the family seemed to prosper, and in 1498, James IV added the titles of hereditary Captain and Keeper of the Rothesay Castle.

After the destruction of Rothesay Castle in 1685 by the 9th Earl of Argyll, the Bute Family lived in the old Mansion House in the High Street, Rothesay. Sir James Stuart was created Earl of Bute in 1703, and the plans were drawn up for the first Mount Stuart, on the present site, in 1716; the house was completed in 1719.

John Stuart, the 3rd Earl of Bute, was passionately interested in both the arts and the sciences. He was a great collector of paintings, particularly seventeenth- and early eighteenth-century Dutch and Italian Renaissance works of art, as well as being a friend and advisor to King George III, a knight of the Garter, 1762, and Prime Minister

Above and below: Mount Stuart Gothic mansion and gardens.

1762–63, although he attracted some prejudices from political opponents during his short time in office.

He was a distinguished botanist, and became the first 'controller' of Kew Gardens; and it was his inspiration that spurred the development of Kew as a botanical garden.In 1780 he became the first President of the Society of Antiquaries in Scotland, and was an important patron to some contemporary craftsmen, architects and painters; such as Alan Ramsey, Robert Adam, and Sir Joshua Reynolds.

He was succeeded by his son, the 4th Earl, who was created Marquess of Bute in 1796. His first wife, whom he married in 1766, was the daughter of Viscount Windsor and Baron Mountjoy, who later inherited great estates in Cardiff and South Wales. His second wife was another heiress, the daughter of Thomas Coutts the banker. His eldest son predeceased him, so at his death in 1814, the 1st Marquess was succeeded by his grandson. The 2nd Marquess (1793–1848) established the family fortune by developing and improving Cardiff Docks – the creator of modern Cardiff.

When the 3rd Marquess of Bute (1847–1900) came of age in 1868, he too became a man of wide interests, a scholar, archaeologist and historian, and a great patron of the arts. He was fascinated with architecture and restoration, and with his architect William Burgess, carried out their fanciful and imaginative ideas on Castell Coch near Tongwynlais and on Cardiff Castle. Bute also restored and recreated historic buildings in Scotland, such as Falkland Palace, Sanquhar Castle and Dunblane Cathedral.

It was sadly ironic, that on 3rd December, 1877, his home, the old Mount Stuart was seriously damaged by fire, apart from the north and south wings. He engaged Scotland's leading expert on Victorian Gothic, Sir Robert Rowand Anderson to design and build a new house on the site. It was fortunate that many of the skilled craftsmen used on the Welsh projects were able to be employed on the new house.

From the ashes of the old Mount Stuart rose a fabulous Gothic palace of intricate splendour and design, which remains today an immoderate statement of architectural flamboyance. When the 3rd Marquess died in 1900, Mount Stuart was unfinished, and much of it was only completed by an ambitious programme of restoration begun in the late 1980s by the 6th Marquess. The work of the programme still continues today.

The house itself

Mount Stuart House, the red sandstone Gothic palace, is one of the most astonishing monuments of the Victorian Age. The basic plan of the main block is a comparatively simple one – a square within a square. The reception rooms are placed on the first floor. There is a fantastic wealth of craftsmanship on show throughout the main rooms of the house: decorated ceilings, rich design and paintwork, heraldic features, fine stained glass, tapestries, sculptures, paintings by famous artists, wood carvings and the use of marble.

The interior of the house offers so much to enjoy. There is a drawing room with an elaborate heraldic ceiling, ornate fireplace over mantel, beautiful stained glass windows and works of art by, or attributed to, Veronese, Titian and Tintoretto. Perhaps the most important feature of the dining room is the outstanding series of eighteenth-century portraits by Thomas Gainsborough, George Romney, Allan Ramsey, Sir Henry Raeburn and Sir Joshua Reynolds.

Stand and look up to admire the impressive height of the Marble Hall, constructed from rare Italian and Sicilian marble and alabaster. Admire the two great tapestries on the walls depicting a Hunting Scene and a Highland Games. The Lady Bute Room, which was originally Lady Bute's sitting room, has a walnut frieze depicting birds and foliage. There is a splendid decorative ceiling of gold ornament upon cedar wood, and heraldic stained glass panels. The red silk wall covering is an original feature of the room.

Mount Stuart today

John, the son of the 6th Marquess is the present head of the Bute family. After a successful career in motor racing, he was British Formula 3 champion in 1984, drove in Formula 1 in the 1986 season and won the Le Mans 24-hour race in 1988, he is now the Chairman of the Mount Stuart Trust. Established in 1989, the Trust undertook to complete the chapel, maintain the buildings and grounds, and open it to the public. Now the 7th Marquess of Bute, he aims to contribute to the local economy by increasing visitor numbers to Mount Stuart, whilst maintaining the rural lifestyle and

natural beauty of the island.

The Mount Stuart Trust has produced an excellent illustrated guidebook of the house and gardens. It contains the history of the Bute Family and Mount Stuart. There is a comprehensive description of the grounds and gardens, and notes of events and facilities for visitors. These include shopping with a range of merchandise, a restaurant and café, an art gallery, educational and conference facilities and a plant centre.

There is also available an informative folding leaflet on the gardens and grounds at Mount Stuart. It contains information on the Kitchen, Wee and Rock Gardens and on four beautiful shorts walks: The Pinetum Walk, 1 Mile (1.6 km); The Garden Walk, 3 miles (4.8.km); The Shore Walk, 2 miles (3.2 km) and The Kerry Trail, $3^{1}/_{2}$ miles (5.6 km).

Entry to Mount Stuart is via the A844 road at the Kerrycroy Bridge, about $^{1}/_{2}$ mile (0.8 km) from Kerrycroy. Visitors from the central part of Scotland and Glasgow can obtain through travel tickets for a day trip using the services of train, boat and bus. These tickets may also include the price of admission to the house and gardens. Car parks, picnic areas and catering facilities are provided for visitors.

KERRYCROY TO ROTHESAY

From Mount Stuart the main road descends to **Kerrycroy**, an attractive estate village with a fine sandy beach. It was designed by Maria North the wife of the 2nd Marquess with houses constructed in the English style. Just to the north of the village on the shoreline are to be found two glacial erratics resting upon a base of old red sandstone. In 1880, when construction of the new Mount Stuart had begun, a railway was laid from the old harbour at Kerrycroy along the shore to enable red sandstone and timber to be carried to the site.

Continue along the coast road to reach the **Ascog Hall Fernery and Gardens**. This splendid award-winning Victorian fern house has been fully restored and replanted, and houses an extensive collection of ferns. It includes one fern that is thought to be 1000 years old, the only survivor from the original collection.

Follow the main road for 1 mile (1.6 km) towards Rothesay, and look out for the sign to **Ardencraig Garden**. The existing gardens originally formed part of a layout for the owners of Ardencraig House. The walled garden has been developed to create a propagation and show area, with an emphasis on the educational side of the horticulture. There are extensive floral displays including fuchsia and bedding sections. As well as views across the Firth of Clyde, there is a selection of foreign birds in spacious aviaries. The gardens can be reached by car, bus or a pleasant walk through

Bogany Wood from Rothesay.

The A844 begins to turn round **Bogany Point** passing the former **Craigmore Pier** building, now a restaurant. By 1837, the pattern of sea transport between Bute, Glasgow and the Ayrshire coast was firmly established. Although Rothesay was the key point for many years the other island piers at Kilchattan Bay, Port Bannatyne and Craigmore had their own share of sea traffic. As road transport on the island improved the piers gradually lost their business. Craigmore was not used after the 1930s.

The road enters Rothesay passing many houses on the hill looking out to sea. There are a considerable number of attractive residences, some of them interesting examples of Victorian architecture and now serving as hotels. Rothesay has many advantages as a holiday centre: its position, accommodation facilities and easy accessibility from the mainland. Nevertheless, the Isle of Bute has a successful agricultural industry, which is an important factor, and which generally enables the island to retain a life of its own. Bute is more than the influence of Rothesay – it is a lovely island of tranquillity, great beauty and wide variety of landscape.

4. Isle of Cumbrae

GREAT CUMBRAE

One thought concerning the origins of the name Cumbrae is that the island derives its name from a Gaelic word meaning, 'safe haven'. The early settlers were mainly farmers and fishermen who lived in a number of small homesteads dotted around the island. In the seventh century Saint Maura established a religious settlement on the island, which was no doubt visited by the Norsemen. The Vikings appear to have left no long lasting impact on the island by way of names or physical features and places.

There is no doubt that any islander on the east side of the island in the thirteenth century, would have had a grandstand view of the Battle of Largs in 1263. King Haakon had not only to fight a running land battle with the Scottish forces, but his fleet of 160 ships were battered by an Atlantic gale sweeping past Arran and the Cumbraes.

A turning point in the history of Great Cumbrae, was when the Clyde Revenue Service began to patrol the Firth of Clyde and stationed a revenue cutter on the island around 1650. This meant that the crewmen and officers began to settle into the Millport area. But it was not until 1797 that a harbour was established, and this saw the population doubling by the mid nineteenth century. The oldest part of Millport centred round the harbour, and houses and buildings soon spread out east and west around the bay. By the end of that century the increase in trade and tourism had necessitated further extensions to the pier.

In the heyday of the Clyde as a tourist area, Millport's population used to double during the summer holiday season. Its accessibility from Glasgow, by train to Largs, and a short ferry ride, meant that visitors could very quickly leave behind the smoke and bustle of the big city. The Clyde pleasure steamers, with a trip 'doon the watter', became a great favourite with visitors. This also provided a source of maritime work for the islanders, as Millport developed into a holiday resort with hotels, boarding houses, bars and entertainment facilities.

MODERN TIMES

But times move in phases as happened on Bute; prosperity marches with decline; the steamers stopped calling, and in more recent times, the expansion of cheap foreign holidays changed people's ideas and expectations. The challenge is to use what is already there, and to capitalise on present-day visitors' extraordinary range of interests and pursuits.

Left: War Memorial – Millport, Great Cumbrae.

Being an island, it was understandable that fishing and shipping were to play an important role in economy. Many islanders were employed on the steamers and during the height of the fishing boom on local fishing boats. The famous Clyde puffers were regular visitors to the island, bringing in coal, timber, building materials and carrying away the island's produce. One famous puffer was the *Saxon*, which served Millport for nearly 40 years. Late in her career the *Saxon* featured as the *Vital Spark* in the original BBC Series of Neil Munro's *Tales of Para Handy*.

Farming

Great Cumbrae was said to be like a piece of mainland Ayrshire, in terms of landscape and in terms of agriculture. The farms tended to be a mix of arable and livestock farming, with potatoes one of the most important crops. There was even a pier called the Tattie Pier, where an early crop was loaded for the mainland markets.

The advent of the 'roll-on, roll-off' ferry service by Caledonian Macbrayne has changed the island's maritime traffic. Visitors from Glasgow and Scotland's populated heartland can easily reach Largs by train. The crossing only takes ten minutes and there is a frequent service to Cumbrae Slip, every 15 minutes in summer and hourly in winter. For foot passengers, a bus awaits to convey them into Millport.

Cumbrae Slip opened in 1972, and for the first time allowed for a regular car ferry service from Largs.

Regular sailings to Millport Pier stopped in 1985, but the paddle steamer *Waverley* calls at Millport during the summer months; there are delightful full or half-day excursions to various places in the Firth of the Clyde.

GEOLOGY

Most of the island of Great Cumbrae is formed of old red sandstone, but the area round Millport has a band of carboniferous sedimentary rocks. There are many igneous dykes, and some of the outstanding features have been given names such as 'The Lion' near the south east corner opposite Largs, and the **Deils Dyke** near Keppel Pier. Down the west coast of the island is a long line of old sea cliffs and raised beaches; the coastal road takes advantage of this level ground. Apart from a small section of coastline in the south east, the remaining coastal strip is formed of deposited material.

As the continents drifted apart, the continental crust was stretched and thinned, which allowed the molten rock to force its way to the surface. This solidified in vertical sheets, or dykes of black dolerite. The Old Red Sandstone tells of a time when flash floods brought down sands and gravels from the mountains and deposited the material on the plains. Thus the red sandstones, pebbly sandstones and conglomerates of Old Red Sandstones were formed.

One of the interesting rock outcrops has become quite famous.

The Crocodile Rock near to Kames Bay at Millport was first painted around 1896 by a retired architect Robert Brown. After rather too many drinks at lunchtime he saw the rock looking like a crocodile. The next day he came back sober with pots of paint and painted the face in red, black and white. The rock has remained painted ever since.

AROUND THE ISLAND

The road around the shoreline of Great Cumbrae was completed in 1875, and ever since, visitors have taken the opportunity to walk, cycle, drive or in the early days, enjoy a horse and trap around the island. The distance around the shoreline, on the B896, is 10¹/₂ miles (16.8 km). The B899 from Kames Bay, Millport to Cumbrae Slip for the ferry to Largs is almost 2¹/₂ miles (3.8 km); a mile (1.6 km) less than via the coast road.

In summer, the road around the island almost rivals Amsterdam, with numerous holidaymakers on cycles in search of exercise and fun. On Great Cumbrae the bicycle is the ideal form of transport. The other circuit of interest to cyclists is the inner circle route. This leaves Millport and climbs up to the island's highest point at the **Glaid Stone on Barbay Hill**, 416ft (127m). From this point there are fine views towards the Argyll and Ayrshire coasts, and westwards to the islands of Bute and Arran.

Continue beyond the Glaid Stone to the mineral spring discovered in 1928. The waters containing iron advanced the belief that Millport could become a spa resort, but sadly, the idea faded and the spring

WALKS ON GREAT CUMBRAE

WALK 1: Farland Point
MAP: OS Explorer 341
DISTANCE: 3¹/₂ miles (5.4 km)

Starting at Millport Pier, there is a walk to Farland Point, via the Crocodile Rock and Kames Bay. There are views to Kaim Hill on the mainland and south to Ailsa Craig. Follow the path round to the road and on the right there is the University Marine Biological Station at Keppel Pier. Note that there is a small museum and aquarium in the main building, open at various times throughout the holiday season.

WALK 2: Circuit from Millport Pier
MAP: OS Explorer 341
Distance: 3¹/₂ miles (5.6 km)

Starting at Millport Pier, walk uphill on the road to the golf course passing the farms of Lower and Mid Kirkton. Bear left at Upper Kirkton along the side of the farmstead, and then left along a track. Walk by the edge of the field and descend to the road at Sheriff's Port. Follow the coastal path towards Doughend Hole and round Portachur headland to the road and return to the starting point.

The Cathedral

It has a superb interior with a plain nave only 40ft (12m) long and 20ft (6m) wide. The chancel is richly decorated and is separated from the nave by a dominant stone screen. This feature embodies strong Butterfield detail, with bands of colour, brass tracery and polished brass gates. On either side are two pillars of Aberdeen granite, which fan out into a tracery of stone. High up, this feature has a large central stone cross. The plain nave is undecorated except for a tiled floor and memorial brasses. The chancel walls are lined with tiles inlaid with different colours. The ceiling has polygonal rafters and is decorated with flowers and ferns of the island from 1851.

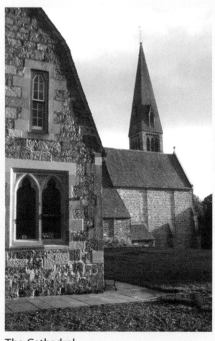

The Cathedral.

The ante-chapel contains two small twentieth-century stained glass windows, and beyond this is the Lady Chapel. The west window of the Cathedral was donated by the workmen as a thank-offering for their safety during the Cathedral's construction. It is of interest to note that this window was blown in by a great storm on Sunday, 28 December 1879.

The spire is 123ft (37.5m) high, and the building was constructed from locally quarried sandstone. This little Cathedral is an architectural gem to be cherished and preserved for the nation; it is the island's treasure.

Looking towards Little Cumbrae from Bute, Torr Mor.

fell into disrepair. The route then descends Tonnel Hill to meet the B899, and the return to Kames Bay and Millport. Then inner circle distance is 4½ miles (7.2.km), but the route can be extended according to individual choice.

The Cathedral of the Isles; and the College of the Holy Spirit

Many visitors seem unaware of the existence of Millport's little **Cathedral**, because it is situated among trees behind the town.

George Frederick Boyle was later to become the 6th Earl of Glasgow, but whilst studying at Oxford in the 1840s, he was carried along by the religious controversies of the time, and became a supporter of the Gothic Revival. As the owner of the Isle of Cumbrae, Boyle commissioned the architect William Butterfield in 1849, to design a college and collegiate church. Butterfield designed a church, two college buildings and a chapter house. The complete community was opened in 1851, although it had students in residence at the end of 1850.

In 1875, the Earl of Glasgow handed over the buildings to the Scottish Episcopal Church, and in 1876, the church was raised to the status of Cathedral of the Isles. It was later in 1920, that St John's Church, Oban became the Cathedral of the United Diocese.

However, in 1885, the Boyle family suffered a financial crash, and their land on Cumbrae and much more was sold. The services in the Cathedral were suspended; but fortunately, the buildings were saved by the intervention of the Diocesan Bishop. The college closed soon afterwards, and it was not until 1946 that it was used for ex-service candidates training for the ministry.

In the intervening years the college was used as a retreat house and then afterwards from 1975 to 1985 it housed an American Order, The Community of Celebration.

The college was re-established as a retreat centre in 1986, and now welcomes church groups and individuals to spend a quiet holiday in this lovely place. It is open all year round, except Christmas and New Year period, and provides accommodation from bed and breakfast to full board for groups and individuals. The house currently enjoys a 3-star guest house rating from the Scottish Tourist Board.

OTHER ATTRACTIONS

Besides the Cathedral and College, Great Cumbrae has much to offer. The **Museum of the Cumbraes** has recently been re-housed behind **the Garrison** (formerly the home of the 6th Earl of Glasgow and scheduled for restoration with grant aid from the Scottish Heritage Lottery Fund).

The **Marine Station** (run by the universities of Glasgow and London) has its own museum and aquarium showing the enormous variety of marine life in the Firth of Clyde. The **Scottish National Water Sports Centre** is situated at Cumbrae Slip. Along with Sportscotland Inverclyde, Largs Yacht Club, Largs Sailing Club and RYA Scotland, Cumbrae forms the **Scottish Sailing Institute**.

Millport has everything to offer for a seaside holiday – sandy beaches, safe bathing, boating and fishing. Cycling is fun on Great Cumbrae and cycles may be hired in the town.

LITTLE CUMBRAE

This small pear-shaped island is 2 miles (3.2 km) long by 1$^1/_2$ miles (2.4 km) wide at its broadest point. It lies half a mile (0.8 km) to the south of Great Cumbrae, and is separated by a narrow stretch of water called **The Tan**. Locally, it is often referred to as 'Wee' Cumbrae, but its past history has involved occupation by hunter gatherers, and evidence certainly indicates Bronze and Iron Age settlement. These have been followed in turn by Celtic missionaries, marauding Vikings, Scottish royalty, tenant farmers and Victorian and Edwardian landowners.

The island has been associated with St Veya, who is thought to have spent her early Christian life with St Cuthbert on Lindisfarne. She wished to find a tranquil setting in the west and travelled to Little Cumbrae to establish her own cell. St Veya is thought to have died in November AD698 on the island, which had become a popular place of pilgrimage.

Little Cumbrae castle was probably built by Walter the Steward, who married the daughter of Robert the Bruce; it was prior to 1375 when the first Royal Charter was signed there. Little Cumbrae castle was broadly constructed to the same plan as strongholds nearby on the mainland; that is an oblong tower keep. As part of the royal hunting area, it does appear to have had its fair share of attacks according to old records. It was set alight in 1445 and burned by Cromwell in 1653.

Excellent details of life on the

island are contained in records of the Cumbrae Historical Society. This was a copy of two volumes of a diary covering the period 1785–1787 which had been kept by Mary Ann Woodrow who had lived on the island. She married a farmer, James Archbald, and they emigrated to the United States in 1807. Her son, who only survived a few days, was buried on Little Cumbrae.

In 1913 Evelyn Stuart Parker became the new owner of Little Cumbrae and set about enlarging the original farmhouse and modifying the garden. He also restored the castle with its walls of considerable strength and thickness. Little Cumbrae House was further altered with the addition of a square tower and a top floor. The ownership of the island has changed hands a number of times through members of Mr Parker's family. Then in 1960, the island was purchased by Mr. Peter Kaye, an entrepreneur, who tried to introduce a hovercraft service for a short while, and in 2002, by another business enterprise.

The situation of Little Cumbrae in the middle of the Firth of Clyde has also proved to be a potential danger to most shipping. With its sharply indented coastline, the island is rugged with many rock outcrops and caves. Finally something had to be done to minimise the threat to shipping, so in 1757 a lighthouse was erected, not on the coast, but on the island's highest point – 404 ft. (123 m). A tower was built to hold a fire of coals burning in an open grate, but the operating difficulties soon became obvious. It would not succeed because coal had to be

carried to the site, the fire kept burning in gales and rainstorms, and someone found to be in charge.

The modern lighthouse on the west coast is automatic and solar powered and has a convenient landing place. Modern-day yachtsmen looking for safe anchorages are warned to steer clear of the north end of the island because of shoals.

From the archaeological point of view the island has a variety of sites and a number of excavations have been recorded, such as cairns hut circles, enclosures, corn kiln, St Veya's Chapel, dykes, field clearance, graveyard, Little Cumbrae Castle, cave and lighthouse.

Apart from two small areas of deposited material along the east and west coasts of Little Cumbrae, the main underlying geological formation is of carboniferous volcanic rocks. Basically, the island is covered with a succession of lava flows and a crossing of the island from east to west allows this sequence to be examined. The land is terraced by a series of lava flows where different kinds of basalt can be distinguished. The earliest flows are exposed along the foreshore near the castle, and the eighth flow, the highest and the thickest, is to be found on Lighthouse Hill.

The new owner of Little Cumbrae feels that the island should be more accessible for visitors, while preserving its unique history, nature and landscape. Great and Little Cumbrae working together can safeguard the future prosperity and well-being of these lovely small islands in the Firth of Clyde.

5. History and Geology

The Ice Age was a prolonged and complex period, with a number of ice-sheets separated by warmer periods in between. The islands were covered in ice during the main glacial period. With a major cooling of the climate about 2.4 million years ago, and the repeated growth and decay of thick ice sheets and glaciers until 10,000 years ago, ice flowed round Arran and Bute, eroding, laying down moraines and cutting U-shaped valleys. The islands were free from ice not much before 8000BC, and by that time, people in the Middle East were already learning to cultivate cereals and to rear sheep and goats.

PRE-HISTORY

The earliest human groups in the Mesolithic Period (c6000BC–4000BC) occupied west central Scotland around 5000BC; evidence has been found of their activities on the raised beaches of the Ayrshire coast and along the gravel terraces of the Clyde. These hunter-gatherers left numerous scatters of flint. About this time, the first colonists reached the islands; perhaps coming from the land around the Mediterranean, and following the Atlantic coastline northwards. Peat deposits show that Arran and Bute were by that time well-wooded islands. Deciduous trees like hazel and oak grew on the better soils, birches on the higher ground, and willows and alders on marshy ground. Also, the rise in the sea level had formed caves in the red sandstone cliffs on Arran, and these may well have provided shelters for the first hunters and fishermen.

In the Neolithic Period (c4000BC–2500BC) the colonists that arrived were accomplished sailors well able to cross short stretches of open water to colonise off-shore islands like Arran, Bute and the Cumbraes. These Neolithic people also brought with them other important skills: the ability to construct large stone/timber monuments and an expertise with cereal crops and the rearing of stock animals. The development of farming was to have a major impact on the environment, regarding population and the felling of the natural tree-cover; hence, the importance of the stone axe. The people would only have tilled small fields, and then probably allowed them to revert back to the forest when fertility decreased. We know little of their houses, but they would probably have been rectangular in shape and of timber construction. However, the important, often surviving feature of this time would be their communal cairns and burial tombs. It is possible that each farming group had its own burial tomb. Today, in some cases, the cairns and tombs now lie in peat-covered areas because of climate change and soil exhaustion.

As time moved into the Bronze Age (c2500BC–700BC) the open land area increased as the forest trees were felled, so the population grew. There was also the significant introduction of metal working, such as copper, gold and bronze. Of particular interest is the know-ledge gained from excavations and study of this period that brought to light homesteads, hut circles and small stone-walled fields. Many archaeological sites including burial cairns, stone circles and standing stones have been discovered, such as the complex of sites at Machrie Moor, Arran.

THE COMING OF THE COLONISTS

With the advent of the Iron Age (c700BC–AD400) the character-istic open settlements of the Bronze Age were gradually replaced by a variety of defended enclosures. These defensive sites differed from area to area, but in the main consisted of extensive banks and steep-sided ditches, the entrance or entrances sealed by wooden gates. In others, dry-stone walls, their interiors filled with earth and rubble, protected the earth banks.

This period in history was partly ushered in by the appearance of Celtic-speaking invaders, first of all reaching southern and then western England. Therefore, it seems that a period of insecurity forced the population to construct a large number of hill forts; and duns as they are known in Scotland. Also, the significant factor of a worsening climate with wetter and cooler weather reduced the amount of agricultural land. This led to increased conflict between the settlements, and the need for fortified enclosures.

The forts were designed to deter humans not animal predators, particularly as some of the Celtic newcomers were well known for cattle raiding. This new order of fortified enclosures, many situated on hill tops or on coastal headlands, although modified, and then briefly interrupted by the Romans, lasted until the arrival of the Normans in the twelfth century.

The main purpose of these fort-ified enclosures was to act as strong-holds to protect the community, their homes and their domestic animals. Life within these forts took on a clan or tribal organisation. The occupants possessed a number of skills: stock rearing, milling flour, pottery making, wool spinning and the crafting of stone and bone tools and implements. An important factor, roughly after 500BC, was the working and use of iron. Iron making required the learning of skills and techniques, as its production is very different from that of bronze. Although the ore was far more easily available and easier to extract than copper or tin, iron was more difficult to forge, hammer and harden. The iron mass from the bloomery furnace could not be cast, but had to be forged and hammered into a required shape. The increased technical ability in iron-making gave the people a great superiority in the production of implements and weapons.

On Bute, a fine example of a vitrified fort is situated at Dunagoil (NS 084 531). Previous excavations have shown that the site was occupied for 300 years by a well-organised community, that fished, and crafted objects. It was found that the inside walls may have been as high as 15ft (4.5m); and that the inhabitants lived in clay and wattle huts, working bronze and iron, using casting moulds and an ore furnace. There were indications of other activities, such as weaving, and the making of bone tools and pottery. The occupants of the forts in Arran and Bute would have possessed domestic animals, such as horses, cattle, goats and sheep, and would have grown barley and other cereal crops.

The comparative isolation of Iron Age Scotland was rudely shattered in AD80; when Agricola led the Roman army northwards from England, and established his authority south of a line from Dumbarton to Stonehaven. A series of forts were established covering the entrances of the main glens from the Highlands. Because their supply and lines of communication became strained, together with trouble back home, it is likely that most of the northern forts were abandoned by AD90.

Following the retreat from Scotland, a defensive line was established from the Solway to the Tyne by the construction of Hadrian's Wall in AD122, in AD138, Emperor Antoninus Pius decreed that southern Scotland should be reoccupied, and that a new defensive line should be built between the Forth and the Clyde. The Antonine Wall was a series of forts and signal posts supported by a road linking with England. This phase of occupation appears to have briefly ended in AD150, then temporarily reoccupied, and finally abandoned not long after AD160.

The islands of Arran, Bute and the Cumbraes appear never to have been included within the Roman Empire, but it is reasonable to accept that their ships would have patrolled the Firth of Clyde. It is also possible that in inclement weather their vessels might have sought shelter in Lamlash Bay on Arran, although there is no evidence to suggest that there was any Roman presence on any of the islands in the Firth of Clyde.

ARRIVAL OF CHRISTIANITY

There is no doubt that Christianity reached the northern frontier of the Roman province well before the occupation of Britain. In the early fifth century, Ninian carried out his missionary work among the southern Picts from his base at Whithorn in Galloway. Probably it was either Ninian or his followers, in the course of further voyages, that set up the chapel at St Ninian's Point on the west of Bute. After excavations were carried out, it appears that this early place of worship was built on the site of former pagan burial grounds. The place was abandoned after Viking raids in the eighth and ninth centuries. Also at this time, the Norsemen raided and burnt the monastery of St Blane's at the southern end of Bute, and the chapel at Kilmichael in the north of the island. Place names give as good an idea of those early visitors; Ninian, Marnoc, Colmac and Blane are among those who have left their names and ruins around the island.

Another early Christian saint was Brendan "the navigator", who roamed the western seas from Ireland to the Orkneys. During his long voyages he may have landed on Arran and Bute – the name Kilbrannen Sound suggests a connection. St Molaise or Molas may have visited Arran to live as a hermit in a cave on Holy Island; in Gaelic – eilean Molaise. Located on the western coast of Arran is the King's Cave between Machrie and Blackwaterfoot. Early visitors had left their marks on the sandstone walls, in the form of a large cross, a rider on horseback, a serpent, a deer and "ogham" inscriptions. These markings form a letter code, probably invented about the time of the introduction of Christianity. Local legend recounts that the adjacent cave was one of the places where Robert the Bruce was fascinated, and in time inspired by, the prolonged efforts of a spider.

Sometime towards the end of the fifth century AD a group of people, called Scotti by the Romans, came over from Northern Ireland (the kingdom of Dalriada) to found a kingdom in the west of Scotland, in what became known as Argyll. They brought a new language, Gaelic, which they introduced into western Scotland. By the late Middle Ages the language had spread throughout most of Scotland north of the Clyde. The spread of Gaelic is graphically illustrated by the study of Gaelic place names, landscape features – headlands, hills, mountains, streams. These names exist at the present day, even where the language, for the most part, has not been spoken for many years.

INTO THE MEDIEVAL PERIOD

It appears that the first recorded Viking raid in the west of Scotland was at Iona in AD 795, followed by many other incursions until the middle of the ninth century. At the onset of the Medieval period many of the Viking descendants had settled as colonists. So by the twelfth century there arose a mixed population of Picts, British, Angles and Vikings that united to form a new Dalriadic kingdom. Dalriada was the old kingdom in Northern Ireland whence the Gaelic-speaking people had originally come. Their first leader was called Somerled; a man of mixed Norwegian and Scottish descent. From this period in time, until Norway sold the Western Isles to Scotland, Somerled's kingdom was, for all intents and purposes, an independent territory.

When the Scottish ruler, Alexander III inherited a kingdom in 1214, it was a territory enlarged by the control of areas most resistant to feudal rule; such as Galloway and the far north. He then turned his attention to the lands held by the Viking/Celtic descendants of Somerled.

On the Isle of Bute, the castle at Rothesay is thought to have been built in the last part of the twelfth century. Its location is close to a safe anchorage in Rothesay Bay. In 1230, the castle was besieged and captured by the Norsemen; and it capitulated again to the Vikings in 1263 prior to the Battle of Largs. There are reasons to believe that it was built by the Scots at an earlier time as a frontier stronghold against the Norsemen.

For the other early settlers, the attraction of Bute lay in its pastoral and sheltered lands. Therefore, for two centuries it was subjected to attacks by Scots and Vikings, and was captured and retaken on a number of occasions. Certainly, after 1230 the island seemed to have become a permanent colony of Norway. However, Alexander III was determined that the islands of the Clyde should return to Scottish rule. The son of Dugall MacSomerled appealed to King Haakon and he sent a fleet of 160 ships to the Clyde. During protracted negotiations, Alexander dragged his feet; and eventually, due to a combination of skilful diplomacy and convenient storms, Haakon was defeated at the Battle of Largs in October 1263. Haakon died two months later in Orkney. In 1266 at the Treaty of Perth, Haakon's successor agreed to sell the Western Isles to Scotland. Bute, Arran and the Cumbraes were brought into the Kingdom of Scotland, by which time the Stewart claim to the islands had the right of feudal authority.

THE HOUSE OF STEWART

The Steward of Rothesay Castle played a leading part with William Wallace at the Battle of Stirling Bridge. As a punishment, Edward I took all the Stewart lands and distributed them to his favourite nobles. After the execution of Wallace who had been treacherously betrayed, Robert the Bruce had himself crowned king at Scone in 1306. On Bute, Rothesay Castle was captured by the English in 1334, also laying waste the island. The castle was used as a royal residence by the house of Stewart; both Robert II and his son Robert III lived there. In 1398 Robert III created his son the Duke of Rothesay; a title still given to the heir to the throne. He also granted a charter to the Borough of Rothesay. The king died in 1406, and the family of the Stewarts became keepers of Rothesay Castle. The title has continued to the present day with the Marquess of Bute still recognised as the Keeper of the Castle.

In the reign on James IV, most of the landholders on the island, who were tenants of Ninian Stewart as Keeper of the Castle, obtained their perpetual leases to the land from the king. Later, Rothesay Castle was considerably improved, and in 1512 began the construction of the great dungeon tower. In the first part of the sixteenth century there were many skirmishes around the castles of Bute and Arran, as well as many raids by the Campbells of Argyll. After James V's death in 1542, Scotland was once again a regency, and the Earl of Lennox invaded Bute and plundered the island. Later, the Campbells attacked Bute, destroying strongholds, murdering the occupants, and executing the provost and important townsmen of Rothesay. During the time of Cromwell, the castle at Rothesay was garrisoned by the Parliamentarians, who later burnt the building and destroyed its defences.

In 1703, the Sheriff of Bute was given a peerage and became the Earl of Bute. This was the first time that the Stewarts held the title, and which has been retained until the present. In 1764, the Earl of Bute began to develop and improve the island's potential; such as the fishing industry, cotton, manufacture and agricultural improvements. In the waters around Bute, Loch Fyne was noted for its great shoals of herring.

As early as the seventeenth century, work was afoot to improve farming on the island. The Earls of Bute were particularly enthusiastic regarding agriculture. There were developments in farmers' courses, on sweetening the soil, on harrowing and on cattle management. A large percentage of farm workers became tenants in their own right; paying great attention to the quality of dairy and beef cattle, and the growing of early potatoes. Certainly, the island's agricultural policy, leading to progress and prosperity, has been and is affected by the strong controlling interest of the Bute family.

During the 1820s, the hydraulics engineer, Robert Thom, increased the flow of water into Loch Fad on Bute, in order to supply the water power for the expanding Rothesay cotton industry. Water was collected by a series of aqueducts following the contours of the land. However, by 1882 the local cotton manufacture was virtually non-existent. Approaching that time, there had been a movement of operatives away to other mills in Lanarkshire.

After the Battle of Bannockburn in 1314, the Isle of Arran once again became the property of the Stewarts. The husband of Robert the Bruce's daughter regained territory on the island, and their son Robert, the grandson of Bruce, was later to become Robert II of Scotland.

Brodick Castle on Arran has a long and interesting history, being destroyed by the English in 1351 and in 1406. In 1467, James III granted the royal lands on the island to Sir Thomas Boyd who was created Earl of Arran, but it appeared to be a temporary appointment. Probably due to court intrigues the lands and titles of the Earls of Arran were forfeited to the crown. However, with an arranged divorce, the Countess of Arran married James, the first Lord Hamilton. Then James, Lord Hamilton's son, was created Earl of Arran in 1503 in the reign of James IV. Again, after a dispute between the Stewarts and the Hamiltons, Brodick Castle was seriously damaged by Ninian Stewart, Sheriff of Bute. James, the son of Ninian Stewart, became a considerable landowner on the island, but in 1549, due to his alliance with the Earl of Lennox, was forced to resign all his lands on Arran.

TROUBLED TIMES

This was the time of the young Queen Mary and her marriage to the dauphin of France, later Francis II. There was hostility from the English, and Arran and the Cumbraes were attacked. Mary returned to Scotland after the death of her husband, and married her cousin, the Earl of Darnley, by whom she had a son, later to be James VI of Scotland and James I of England. Darnley was murdered by the Earl of Bothwell, whom she married three months later. Intrigue followed intrigue, and Mary fled to England in 1568 where she was imprisoned by Elizabeth I. Catholic supporters plotted to place her on the throne of England, and this resulted in her trial and execution.

In 1572, during this unsettled time in Scotland, Lord Arbroath one of the younger brothers of the Earl of Arran was created the 1st Marquess of Hamilton by James VI. Scotland and England were united when James VI of Scotland succeeded Elizabeth in 1603 as James I of England. In the meantime, a Campbell raiding party seized Brodick Castle, but they were attacked by Arran islanders loyal to the Hamiltons. On another occasion the island folk suffered retaliation and their goods and livestock were carried away. After the execution of Charles I, Brodick Castle was occupied by the Parliamentarians. During their stay, the garrison built extensions at both the east and west ends of the castle. Never popular, Cromwell's forces were frequently attacked by the local population.

The 2nd Duke of Hamilton was followed by his niece, Anne, who became Duchess of Hamilton after her marriage with William Douglas who took on the Hamilton name. Anne died in 1716, having supported the Presbyterian church and established it on the island.

FARMING IN DECLINE

The Clearances could be said to be one of the consequences of the Jacobite defeat in 1745. However, at that time land changes were being carried out for what were considered economic and agricultural reasons. The people of Arran had continued to farm the land as part of their traditional Gaelic way of life. They were subsistence farmers operating the runrig, or running share method of farming. The people of each communal clachan, which was a compact collection of dwellings, worked as a community on their shares of the land. They worked on their own plots, and in turn, worked on their neighbours' shares during the course of the day. An annual fixed rent was collected from each family.

From the landowner's point of view, the desire for agricultural improvement led to discoveries in respect of drainage, new crops, crop rotation, improving the soil with lime, the use of new implements and the selective breeding of animals. All this technical progress was achieved at the expense of social justice.

Around 1766, two agrarian advisers, John Burrel and Boyd Anderson, were commissioned to make plans for the introduction of a new style of farming on the Duke of Hamilton's lands in Arran. Eventually, this enclosure and division of the land, the replacement of the clachans, the competition between tenants and the payment of higher rents, meant that people were deprived of access to land. Efforts were made to provide other employment; such as kelp collection, fishing and potato growing which did absorb some of the spare labour. Some families left the island to find work on the mainland where the industrial revolution had begun.

However, the creation of farms for sheep particularly in north Arran, and in the north-west of the island for deer, involved more people displacement. By 1829, the first numbers of emigrants embarked at Lamlash for a new life in southern Canada. Here, they settled on virgin land, clearing the forest, and successfully establishing a thriving Scottish community.

On the death of the 12th Duke of Hamilton, the lands in Arran passed to Lady Mary Louise, who married the Marquess of Graham in 1900. On her death in 1957, the castle and gardens at Brodick passed to the National Trust for Scotland. In fact, most of the estate lands belonging to the Hamiltons have been disposed of. The mountain of Goatfell and the Glen Rosa area were also presented to the National Trust for Scotland.

GEOLOGY

The Isle of Arran is often known as "Scotland in miniature". Since James Hutton, hailed as the founder of modern geology, visited the island in 1787 it has proved to be a fascinating location for investigation and discussion – a place to excite all geologists.

EARLY VOLCANIC ACTIVITY

The granite peaks in the north of Arran are without doubt the most prominent. About sixty million years ago the mass of North America and surrounding blocks were part of the British Isles. The two continents, Europe and America, began to drift apart and cracks appeared in the crust along the west coast of Scotland, including the Firth of Clyde. As the earth's crust thinned, molten rock or magma, forced its way through the weak points. Nearer the surface, the magma cooled into a crystalline rock called granite. Because it cooled slowly, the crystals had time to form. These minerals can easily be recognised as quartz, mica and feldspar.

When the volcanic intrusions took place, the magma forced its way past the existing ancient sedimentary rocks, such as Old Red Sandstones. As the volcanic material was harder, it withstood the agents of denudation, the erosive forces of wind, frost and ice, and stood up as higher ground. When granite cools, like all igneous rocks, it develops cracks and joints. These towers of stone, piled high like giant stone walls called tors, are distinctive features in the landscape. The Arran granite is basically pale grey in colour.

In central Arran, lying on the south side of the road leading from Brodick to Shiskine, are a number of rounded hills, such as Ard Bheinn, 1,680ft (512m), less dramatic than the north. The igneous rocks form the outside of this oval-shaped area, but the centre is occupied by masses of fragments of various kinds of rock. It would appear that these fragments of marls, shales and limestone fell into the vent of the old volcano, or, have been forced up from below.

When a volcano erupts, quite often the molten rock travels sideways between layers of sedimentary rock, such as sandstone. These layers of hard igneous rock consisting of a dark dolerite or a light-coloured felsite are called sills. So the land is formed of alternating hard sills and hollows of softer rocks in between. This stepped landscape constitutes the south part of Arran, and features numerous waterfalls where the water cascades over the hard layers of rock, for example, Glen Ashdale.

The coastline of Arran is also noted for its headlands and fine cliffs, such as Brown Head, Drumadoon and Holy Island; all the result of volcanic sills. Another effect in the stretching of the earth's crust from east to west, was that cracks formed running north to south. The volcanic magma flowed up from the depths, and solidified as vertical sheets or dykes consisting of black dolerite. Because the dykes are harder, they tend to stand out above the sandstone. Along the south coast of Arran the parallel dykes run out to sea with sandy areas in between. In earlier times, the sea level fell, and the dykes eroded by the sea now stand on raised beaches. On the island of Great Cumbrae, some of the dykes stand out as wall-like features, such as the Lion Rock and Diel's Dyke.

CARBONIFEROUS PERIOD

Volcanoes erupted during the Carboniferous period in the Firth of Clyde region, and covered the area with extremely thick layers of lava. In the south end of Bute, one of the striking series of ridges of this volcanic period is Torr Mór, 489ft (149m). It ranges north-west and its scarped edge faces to the north-east. The thickness of the volcanic flow is quite great with the beds repeated several times by faults. One of the main lines of fault is along Glen Callum. All of Little Cumbrae is covered with lava flows, and at least eight main flows can be distinguished. In effect, the entire volcanic sequence can be examined.

At the southern end of Bute near Kilchattan Bay is a large patch of columnar sandstone. It outcrops on the shore, and forms the raised beach cliff near to the end of the road. The vertical columns are crystalline in form, indicating their change as the result of intense heat. There is a weathered dyke nearby. In the Dunagoil area at the south-west tip of Bute, there are basalt cliffs and pillar lava that may be likened to the formation at the Giant's Causeway in Northern Ireland. At Ettrick Bay, a basalt trap dyke runs out to sea just to the west of the mouth of St Colmac Burn.

There are ancient folded rocks such as sandstones, limestones, mudstones and siltstones that were laid down some six hundred million years ago. One hundred million years later the continents collided, which produced great earth movements resulting in the formation of a great mountain chain. The remnants of these mountains are seen today in North America and in the Scottish highlands. These old rocks that have been twisted and severely heated to form quartzites and schists can be found in north Arran and in north Bute. Although they have been worn down to their roots, these ancient rocks form the band of rounded hills around the volcanic core in north Arran, and have also created the craggy uplands to the north and south of a line from Ettrick Bay to Kames Bay in Bute.

The edge of the ancient Highland rocks traverses Bute between Rothesay Bay and Scalpsie Bay; then across to Glen Sannox, and continues just south of the granite in central Arran towards the west coast. This is called the Highland Boundary Fault. The valley formed across the island of Bute contains two fresh-water lochs, Loch Fad and Loch Quien. Here, along the fault line, it is interesting to note the contrast in the landscape: to the north there are craggy uplands; to the south there is more gentle scenery of fertile farmland.

The sedimentary rocks with their layered strata were worn down more rapidly by denudation, and they form the lower ground in the southern part of Arran. On Bute they form the central part between the northern hills and the Carboniferous lava hills in the south.

The Old Red and New Red Sandstones give a number of clues as to the environment in which they were formed. They tell of a time when torrential floods washed down sand and pebbles from the Caledonian mountains, and deposited the material in the plains. Winds blew the sands into dunes, and so eventually, the red and pebbly sandstones were formed. However, the warmth of Permian times with its tropical seas finished abruptly with the coming of the Ice Age.

THE ICE AGE

During this time, a number of ice sheets and glaciers covered Scotland. The ice moved south from the Highlands leaving its telltale striations on the rocks and boulders and wearing down the softer rocks. It gouged out hollows in the Kyles of Bute and carved out U-shaped valleys on Arran, such as Glen Sannox and Glen Rosa. The mountain slopes were eroded by the action of ice and frost into hollows called corries. Sharp mountain ridges like A'Chir on Arran were formed when the slopes were eroded on both sides.

On the north side of Ettrick Bay in west Bute Glen More is a typical example of a U-shaped valley that was scooped out by the gouging and grinding of melting ice. Rocks and boulders were rounded and scratched by ice-action, and sometimes carried away long distances from their source; these are known as erratics. Rock specimens from Ailsa Craig have even been discovered in South Wales. In Bute, there is a large boulder on the shore at Ettrick Bay. This mass of dolerite was carried by a glacier from the head of Glen More, and left perched on a bed of mica schist. Piles of debris were deposited along the sides or on the valley floor. These banks or mounds of detritus consisting of ground up rock, stones, clay and boulders are called moraines.

Right at the end of the Ice Age, dating back to a time of around 6000 years, the sea level was higher than it is now. It is interesting to note that at this time, particularly at high tide, Bute was composed of three islands. As the world's sea level has fluctuated with the increase and decrease of the ice caps, so there are features and deposits along the coastlines of the islands in the Firth of Clyde. These features are at varying heights corresponding with the sea levels at particular times and are known as raised beaches, level areas a few feet above the sea level, backed by a line of cliffs that contain caves at different levels. A well-known cave is the King's Cave on the west coast of Arran. There are also sand and shingle beach deposits, wave-cut platforms in the rock, and rock columns called sea-stacks. So, the features associated with raised beaches are found not only on Arran, but on Bute, Inchmarnock, Great Cumbrae and Little Cumbrae.

FACT FILE

GETTING THERE AND GETTING AROUND

Fact File

General information

Traveline
information on all public transport
☎ 08706 082608
www.traveline.org.uk

Scotrail
☎ 08457 484950
www.scotrail.co.uk

Scottish Citilink Coaches
☎ 08705 505050
www.citylink.co.uk

Caledonian MacBrayne
General enquiries & car ferry reservations
☎ 08705 650000

Timetable information (24 hours)
☎ 01631 566966

On-line information
and reservations
www.calmac.co.uk

Arran

The Isle of Arran is very accessible by roll-on roll-off ferry from Ardrossan on the Ayrshire coast. Crossing time is one hour. Ardrossan ferry terminal ☎ 01294 463470. Brodick ferry terminal ☎ 01770 02166.

From the south, via Carlisle, it is an easy drive to Ardrossan, and the train service direct from Glasgow Central to Ardrossan Harbour takes just under the hour. Visitors arriving by air at Prestwick International Airport can reach Ardrossan by train, changing at Kilwinning. From Glasgow Airport, the ferry train from nearby Paisley Gilmour Street is the best option. The ferry sails to Brodick and the service is operated by Caledonian MacBrayne Ltd, who run the service all year round.

There is a summer service between Lochranza (Arran) and Claonaig (Kintyre) that takes 30 minutes, and in the winter from Lochranza to Tarbert (Kintyre) 1 hour 25 minutes. During the summer months, the last sea-going paddle steamer, the *Waverley*, runs day cruises from Brodick and the Ayr coast around the Firth of Clyde (☎ 0845 130 4647, ☎ 0141 2218152, www.pswaverley.org.uk).

Bus services on the island are operated by Stagecoach Western, Arran Depot, The Pier, Brodick KA27 8AU. ☎ 01770 302000
Services operate from:-
Brodick – Corriegills
Brodick – String Road – Blackwaterfoot
Brodick – Whiting Bay – Blackwaterfoot

Fact File

Brodick – Lochranza – Blackwaterfoot
North Island Circle
South Island Circle
Island Circles
Royal Mail – Postbus Services:-
North Island Circular
Arran Circular
South Island Circular

Bute

There are regular 35-minute car ferry crossings from Wemyss Bay (pronounced Weems) to Rothesay (Rothesay ferry terminal ☎ 01700 502707); also 5-minute journeys from Colintraive to Rhubodach. There are train services from Glasgow Central to Wemyss Bay. Visitors flying in to Glasgow Airport on national and international flights can catch the train from Paisley Gilmour Street Station to Wemyss Bay. From Prestwick International Airport, the journey to Wemyss Bay by car takes 60 minutes, or by train to Paisley and thence to the ferry terminal at Wemyss Bay (☎ 01475 520521).

Bus services on Bute ☎ 01546 6004360

Great Cumbrae

Visitors from Glasgow and Scotland's populated heartland can easily reach Largs by train. The crossing by car ferry to Great Cumbrae only takes ten minutes and there is a frequent service to Cumbrae Slip, every 15 minutes in summer and hourly in winter(Largs ferry terminal ☎ 01475 674134). For foot passengers, a bus awaits to convey them into Millport.

ACCOMMODATION

There are many hotels, guest houses, bed and breakfasts and self-catering units on Arran, Bute and Great Cumbrae. Full details can be obtained from the Tourist Information Centres at Rothesay, Brodick, Millport and at the National Booking and Information Centre.

Caravan and camping sites

Roseland
Rothesay
Bute
☎ 01700 504529

**Seal Shore camping
and touring site**
Arran
☎ 01770 820320
mdeighton@sealshore.fsnet.co.uk

BANKS

Clydesdale
Rothesay
☎ 01700 503134

Royal Bank of Scotland
Brodick
☎ 01770 302222

Bank of Scotland
Millport
42 Stuart Street
☎ 0845 7801801

Bank of Scotland
Brodick
☎ 0845 7801801

BOOKS ABOUT THE ISLANDS

Bellamy M, *Millport and the Cumbraes* (Tempus 2003)
British Geological Survey, *Arran and the Clyde Islands* (Scottish
Natural Heritage (1997))
Buteshire Natural History Society, *Island Trails*
Campbell JRD, *A Peep into Little Cumbrae's Past* (2004)
Fairhurst H, *Exploring Arran's Past* (Brodick, 1982)
Footprint, *The Isle of Bute – West Island Way* (2005)
Haswell–Smith H, *The Scottish Islands* (Canongate 2004)
History and Guide Book, *Cathedral of the Isles and College of
the Holy Spirit*
Marshall DN, *History of Bute* (1992)
McLellan R, Revised by Newton N, (Pevensey Press 1995)
McLellan R, *The Isle of Arran* (David and Charles 1985)
Mount Stuart, Isle of Bute, The Mount Stuart Trust (2001)
Munro IS, *The Island of Bute* (David and Charles 1973)
Newton NS, *The Isle of Bute* (Pevensey Press 1999)
Ritchie G, Harman M, *Exploring Scotland's Heritage, Argyll and
the Western Isles* (HMSO 1985)
Scottish Women's Rural Institute, *Arran, History of the Villages of
the Isle of Arran* (2002)
Stevenson JB, *Exploring Scotland's Heritage, The Clyde Estuary
and Central Region* (HMSO 1985)

CHURCHES

Arran Free Church
Shiskine
☎ 01700 502047

St Andrews Catholic
Rothesay
☎ 01700 502781

Cathedral of the Isles
Millport
☎ 01475 530353

CYCLE HIRE

Brodick Cycles
Brodick
☎ 01770 302460

Boathouse Gifts
Brodick
☎ 01770 302868

Bremners
Millport
☎ 01475 530309,
or 01475 530707

Morton
Millport
☎ 01475 540478

DOCTORS

Brodick
☎ 01770302175

Lamlash
☎ 01770600516

Shiskine
☎ 01770 860247

Bute Health Practice
Rothesay
☎ 01700502290

Millport
☎ 01475 530329

EMERGENCY NUMBERS

In an emergency ring 999, otherwise

Police

Millport
Isle of Cumbrae
☎ 01475 530316

Rothesay
Isle of Bute
☎ 01700 894000

Lamlash
Isle of Arran
☎ 01770 302573

Strathclyde
Dunoon
☎ 01369 763000

Strathclyde HQ
Glasgow
☎ 0141 5322000

Lifeboat

Lamlash Pier
Isle of Arran
☎ 01770 600250

GARAGES

Angus Lambie
Brodick
☎ 01770 302677, 01770 302568

Bute Motor Co.
Rothesay
☎ 01700 502330

Blackwaterfoot
Shiskine, Arran
☎ 01770 860277, 01770 860285

McKirdy & McMillan
Rothesay
☎ 01700 502317

Whiting Bay Garage
Arran
☎ 01770 700345

Horn RK
Millport
☎ 01475 530567

GOLF

Golf clubs on the islands:

Brodick (18 hole)
☎ 01700 302349

Whiting Bay (18)
☎ 01770 700487

Corrie (9)
☎ 01770 810606

Bute (9)
☎ 01700 502158

Lamlash (18)
☎ 01770 600296

Port Bannatyne (13)
☎ 01700 504544

Lochranza (18)
☎ 01770 830273

Rothesay (18)
☎ 01700 503554

Machrie Bay (9)
☎ 01770 840259

Millport (18)
☎ 01475 530306

Shiskine (12)
☎ 01770 860226

Further details of all these
courses can be found on
www.scottishgolfsouthwest.com

MAPS

OS Explorer Series Nos. 361, 362, 341

PLACES TO VISIT

Arran

Arran Heritage Museum
Brodick
☎ 01770 302636
www.arranmuseum.co.uk
Open daily, April to October

Paterson Arran Ltd
Lamlash
☎ 01770 600606
kitchen and farm shop
open all year

Fact File

Brodick Castle
☎ 01770 302202
www.nts.org.uk
Open daily, April to October

Arran Chocolate Factory
Brodick
☎ 01770 302873

Arran Brewery
Brodick
☎ 01770 302353
www.arranbrewery.co.uk
Open all year

Isle of Arran Distillery
Lochranza
☎ 01770 830264
www.arranwhisky.com
Open March to December

Arran Cheese Shop
Brodick
☎ 01770 302788
open all year

Arran Aromatics
Home Farm
Brodick
☎ 01770 302595
www.arranaromatics.com

Crafts of Arran
Whiting Bay
☎ 01770 700251

Torrylinn Creamery
Kilmory
☎ 01770 870240

Bute

Ardencraig Gardens & Aviary
☎ 01700 504644
open May to September

Ascog Hall Fernery & Gardens
☎ 01700 504555
open Easter to end of October

The Bute Museum
☎ 01700 505067
open all year

Mount Stuart House & Gardens
☎ 01700 503877
www.mountstuart.com
Open Easter and May to
September

Rothesay Castle
☎ 01700 502691
open all year

Rothesay Creamery
☎ 01700 503186

Rothesay Discovery Centre
☎ 01700 502151

Ardbeg Bowling Club
☎ 01700 502164

Loch Fad Fishery
☎ 01700 504871

Great Cumbrae

Wildlife and Island Adventures
From Millport Pier
☎ 0845 2570404
www.cumbraevoyages.co.uk

Cathedral of the Isles
☎ 01475 530353
tccumbrae@argyll.anglican.org
www.scotland.anglican.org/
retreats

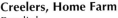

RESTAURANTS

Creelers, Home Farm
Brodick
☎ 01700 302810

Joshua's Café & Bistro
Whiting Bay
☎ 01770 700308

Mac's Bar
Brodick
☎ 01770 302531

Stalkers Eating House
Brodick
☎ 01770 302579

Taj Mahal Tandoori
Lamlash
☎ 01770 600600

The Wine Port
Whiting Bay
☎ 01770 700489

An Cala
Rothesay
☎ 01700 502324

Bistro – Bute Discovery Centre
Rothesay
☎ 01700 505500

Brechin's Brassierie
Rothesay
☎ 01700 502922

India Pavilion Tandoori
Rothesay
☎ 01700 504988

Jade Garden
Rothesay
☎ 01700 502347

Pier at Craigmore
Rothesay
☎ 01700 502867

Spice Island Tandoori
Millport
☎ 01475 530900

Minstrels Wine Bar
Millport
☎ 01475 531080

PONY TREKKING

North Sannox
Arran
☎ 01770 810222

South Bank Farm
Kildonan
Arran
☎ 01770 820221

Kingarth Trekking Centre
Kilchattan Bay
Bute
☎ 01700 831673

TOURIST INFORMATION CENTRES

Rothesay
Isle of Bute
☎ 08707 200619
info@rothesay.visitscotland.com

Brodick Pierhead
Arran
☎ 01770 302140

**Scotland's National Booking
and Information Centre**
☎ 0845 2255121
info@visitscotland.com

Index